MW00623058

COPYRIGHT

THANK YOU GIFT

As a thank you gift to my readers, I have a little surprise I hope you will enjoy...

A FREE Copy of one of our newest and most exciting books! *"WORLD WONDERS: A Captivating Compilation Of Random Trivia, Fascinating Facts, And Curious Tidbits To Catch The Quick-Witted Off Guard"*

YOUR FREE BOOK – Upcoming Code!

"WORLD WONDERS: A Captivating Compilation Of Random Trivia, Fascinating Facts, And Curious Tidbits To Catch The Quick-Witted Off Guard"

WORLD WONDERS

To obtain your **FREE** copy of ***WORLD WONDERS***
- Scan The Code Below, Or Simply Head to:

https://bit.ly/WORLDWONDERSFREE

READ OUR NEWEST BOOKS AT NO COST BEFORE THEY HIT THE SHELVES

Are you an avid reader who loves being the first to discover the latest bestsellers? Joining Advanced Reader Copy (ARC) teams gives you the exclusive opportunity to read books before they hit the shelves! Not only do you get to enjoy the excitement of being among the first to read new releases, but you also have the chance to provide valuable feedback to authors and publishers, helping to shape the final version of the book. The best part is, you'll receive each and every single one for *free*. So, if you want to be at the forefront of the literary world and have a say in the next big

thing, sign up to our ARC team today!

UPCOMING ARC

Scan the upcoming code for details. Or, simply head to

https://owenjanssenarc.com/

contact me

If you enjoy reading this book, I would be so appreciative if you took the time to leave a review in your respective marketplace.

It means the world to authors such as myself. Or, if you would like to chat with me directly, I would love to hear from you! *Contact me at* **support@owenjanssen.com** *or head to* **owenjanssen.com**.

BETTER THAN BALDERDASH

The Ultimate Collection of Incredible True Stories, Intriguing Trivia, and Absurd Information You Didn't Know You Needed

Owen Janssen

contents

PROLOGUE

You might think that the Roman Colosseum is degrading simply because of its age. Oh, it is very old, but you would have never guessed that it was actually covered in marble at one point. When the fall of Rome happened, the Goths looted the marble and stripped the structure down to its bare stone setting. This has caused it to age faster, but what about those pockmarks? That comes from where the Goths would anchor themselves to the structure to chip the marble off!

Did you know that one of those inexpensive singing birthday cards has more computing power than the entire Allied army did during World War II? They'd probably be astonished at what actual computing power we have today.

If you knew those, did you also know that the snow in the poppy field scene in *Wizard of Oz* was actually asbestos-based snowflakes? How about the famous U.S. president Abraham Lincoln being in the Wrestling Hall of Fame?

There are so many interesting facts out there in the world, from history to pop culture; and, back before we had the internet, there were so many trivia books. I believe they were called "bathroom readers" or "pub-style trivia" books.

Now, we have websites, trivia nights at bars, and even social media sites to pick up unbelievable facts. My love of trivia started before all of that, when we still had those "bathroom readers." I do, however, still love falling down the rabbit hole of reading lists of amazing facts.

I remember moving to the United States with my parents when I was a kid. We seemed to be stuck in the car for hours as we traversed the country. Whether it was traveling to the next city where my father was working, going on vacations, or visiting family for the holidays, there was a lot of time spent in cars, planes, hotels, and relatives' houses. This meant that between my mother, two other children, and myself, we had to stay entertained or we'd drive my father crazy.

My mom always packed the trivia books, or my dad would rattle off his own trivia (a lot of which my mom didn't approve of). We turned it into a game. At the very least, it sparked some interesting conversations about random facts. Trivia helped to pass a lot of time, but it also became the thing that fascinated me the most.

Even as the years went on, I still held on to those books. That's how I made friends at whichever school I ended up in. Hey, you can't deny a good icebreaker like trivia!

As I got older and went to college, I always kept the latest edition of a trivia book in my dorm room. I think the books acted as my security blanket against the unknown. Even with the new adventure of college life, I remained the guy breaking the ice with random trivia at parties. It worked well! The first thing I said to my future wife was about "Psycho" being the first movie in America to feature a toilet flushing; and the rest, as they say, is history.

When I studied abroad and later traveled the world, I learned even more random facts in all the different countries. I still couldn't move on from the books, though. They were the things that brought me the most comfort. I always had one, and I'd open it up whenever I was feeling homesick while stuck in my hotel room.

In time, I stopped using my trivia books because I wasn't finding anything interesting or new anymore.

As a teacher, it is important to connect with the kids in your class. That's not always easy to do, but I realized that trivia could, once more, come to the rescue. I started each class with a greeting and one random trivia question. I could see the kids' reactions, though. Years ago, I pulled the same face when I realized that trivia books had a cut-off date. It seemed like there were no new discoveries. Some of the facts showed their age, and the political landscape had changed greatly.

Kids don't hold back, either. "Mr. Janssen, did anything happen after 1986?" "Did they not update this stuff?" "Just how old are you?"

I couldn't argue with their complaints. After all, these books were as old as I was. I knew it was difficult for the writers because some historical facts can only be repeated so much before it's not that amazing any longer. But, you also can't ignore current trends, or your book will be useless in two to three years.

As a joke, my students started telling me I should write a trivia book of my own. It was an interesting but crazy idea, so I talked myself out of it. It wasn't until my wife reminded me of how we met that it dawned on me that it might not be such a bad idea, after all.

My passion project began with choosing a title. That proved to be quite the challenge!

I know some of you saw the title and probably thought, "Who says *balderdash* anymore?" My students love words that aren't bad, but sound like they could be. *Balderdash* just happens to be their favorite. They say it reminds them of an older gentleman with a large mustache and a pipe.

Of course, you want to know if this is really better than balderdash. Why wouldn't it be? These facts will leave you feeling as if they couldn't possibly be real. I assure you, they may sound bizarre, but they are very much real.

BETTER THAN BALDERDASH

After having read this book, you'll be ready to host your own game nights at home and astound your coworkers and friends with your new wealth of knowledge!

CHapTer 1: WorLD HisTory

Pepsi once supplied the Soviet Union with soda in exchange for a naval fleet.

One of the craziest bits of knowledge is that the soda company Pepsi once had a bigger naval fleet than many global powers. In the early 1990s, just before the Soviet Union dissolved, Pepsi struck a bizarre deal with the Russians. The Soviet Union wanted to have Pepsi in their country, and warships were the only instruments they had to pay for it. Pepsi ended up with 17 submarines, a cruiser, a frigate, and a destroyer.

A Soviet lieutenant colonel, Stanislav Petrov, prevented a global nuclear war in the 80s.

Stanislav Yevgrafovich Petrov had his action hero moment in 1983 when he prevented what would have been a catastrophic nuclear war. While at the command center for the Oko nuclear early warning system, Petrov was alerted to a nuclear missile incoming from the United States. The first missile was followed by five more. The Soviet protocol, if followed, would have seen the

USSR launch a nuclear attack of its own against the US. However, Petrov disobeyed orders and called the alert a false alarm. Lucky for us, he was right. The Soviet satellite that detected attacks had malfunctioned and there were no incoming missiles.

King Mithridates IV from Pontus, a small kingdom in the Black Sea, stopped a Roman invasion by using wild animals as the attackers.

When Rome was at war with the Mithridates, the Romans were trying to invade Themyscira. The fortress walls were too high for them to scale, so the Romans got crafty and dug tunnels beneath the city. Upon seeing how successful the Romans were at this, the defenders dug a few tunnels of their own. These trenches, however, were not meant for brave warriors. The Mithridates sent bees and other wild animals, including bears, into the tunnels to attack the Romans and stop them in their tracks.

In 1816, there was no summer.

After one of the biggest and deadliest volcanic eruptions in history, an immense amount of dust, ash, and sulfur dioxide was released into the air. That shielded Earth from the sun, thereby "canceling" summer that year.

One war lasted over a century because both sides forgot they were still in a war.

During a war between Russia and Japan in 1904-1905, volunteers from Montenegro fought on the side of the Russian Army. The peace treaty that ended the war, unfortunately, left out one minor detail. Montenegro was not mentioned once, so technically, the country was still involved in a war with Japan.

Long ago, people accidentally buried alive could save themselves by ringing a bell.

Medicinal practices in the Middle Ages were quite primitive compared to today. Proof of this is the number of people mistakenly buried alive when they were only comatose. To counteract this, people were buried with a string attached to one of their hands. The string was tied to a bell outside the grave. Anyone waking up from a coma to find themselves buried could tug the string to ring the bell. That would alert people to come and dig them up. This practice is the origin of our expression "saved by the bell."

Herostratus, a 4th-century B.C.E. Greek, was possibly the first infamous person in history.

What did he do to get this notoriety? Well, he burned down the Temple of Artemis for the sole reason of becoming famous. These acts led to the creation of a *damnatio memoriae* law, which forbade anyone to speak his name. He is, however, mentioned in modern works, so he ultimately got his way. It just goes to show that some people can't stop talking about bad people.

The Polish military adopted a bear cub who became a mascot for the war.

Polish soldiers one day found a Serbian brown bear cub while on patrol during WWII and took the animal back to camp with them. They raised him on milk, but the bear, named Wojtek, quickly developed the soldiers' habits. He joined them in smoking by taking a puff of a cigarette and then swallowing the whole thing. Wojtek also loved drinking beer with the soldiers and attending military dances. The cub soon became a mascot for the soldiers, reaching the rank of corporal and receiving his own military patch. During battles, Wojtek carried ammo to the troops. After the war, he lived the rest of his relatively long life as a normal bear, despite his wartime vices.

There is a piece of Scandinavian gum that is around 10,000 years old.

Chewing gum is found everywhere today, including under the desks of school children. But, this item has been around longer than many of us would have imagined. While studying gum made of birch bark tar that was close to 10,000 years old at the time, researchers discovered Scandinavian DNA on it. That means people had been chewing gum for millennia already .

There once was a dancing plague.

In 1518, an illness ran rampant over a city which was part of the Holy Roman Empire. The citizens of Strasbourg didn't cough or sneeze, though. They were infected by dancing! The dancing plague lasted for weeks. About 400 infected people danced until their feet bled. Some of them died from heart attacks and strokes, while others died from pure exhaustion. No one is exactly sure what caused the bizarre phenomenon, even today. It has been speculated that it could have been mold or perhaps simply the first well-documented outbreak of mass hysteria.

The first female mayor in U.S. history got into office because of a joke.

The United States and bizarre politics seem to go hand in hand. In the state of Kansas, before women had the right to vote, Susanna Salter was a member of the temperance movement in the town of Argonia. That irritated the local men and they decided to try and humiliate her by putting her on the mayoral ballot. They assumed she'd lose in a landslide and become a laughing stock. The joke was on them, though. Susana took up the challenge and started canvassing votes. She won the election to become the first female mayor in U.S. history.

Ancient Greece probably started the world's misconception about redheads.

Redheaded people, or "gingers," are sometimes ridiculed for having no soul. This stems from a belief in Ancient Greece that redheads would turn into vampires after death. Vampire folklore was alive and well in Greek mythology and, unlike the bronze skin of the Greeks, redheads were (and still usually are) very pale skinned.

Pineapples once were regarded as a status symbol.

This tropical fruit didn't make its way to England's shores until the 1600s, but before the century was over, pineapples had become a craze. Clothes, housewares, and many other items were decorated with pineapples. If you were wealthy enough, you could afford to buy a pineapple to show you were high-class. Poorer people could rent one for a day, instead.

The US considered using bats to help them win WWII.

Something about wartime and animals just seems to go hand in hand. When America finally entered WWII, a dentist convinced the American president to bomb Japan with armed bats. The plan was moving along well until some of the bats were released accidentally, destroying the testing facility.

The Roman emperor Elagabalus, officially known as Antoninus, ran one very cruel lottery.

Augustus Caesar created a lottery for the Roman people. The prizes offered included things like houses or slaves. The money raised was used to fund government projects, just like today. When Elagabalus took over as emperor, the lottery turned sinister. He catapulted lottery tickets, along with some instant prizes, into the crowds. The instant prizes were venomous snakes. By the time his brief reign ended, the prizes had devolved into dead animals, wasps, bees, or even death sentences. One can't help but wonder why anyone was still taking part in it.

During the Great Depression, couples used dance competitions to get shelter and food for awhile.

The Great Depression was a dark time for most people. They were out of money, and some were also homeless. Both the economy and the people were in a depression. To raise spirits, there were sponsored "dance-till-you-drop" competitions. Many of these couples only took part for a chance to be under a sturdy roof for a while. Food was served as well, so they could get something to eat at the same time. If one or both partners stopped dancing, they were eliminated. To get around this, one partner would prop the sleeping party up and dance with them to give them some rest.

A Mexican general gave his leg a hero's burial.

General Antonio Lopez de Santa Anna of Mexico, who called himself the "Napoleon of the West," was wounded seriously in a battle against the French in Veracruz in 1839. The only way to save the general's life was to amputate his mangled leg. The general had the leg buried on his estate, but felt it received only a peasant's funeral. He made sure it was dug up and buried beneath a monument fit for a decorated general. The second burial only took place after the leg paraded through Mexico City with military honors, poetry readings, and cannon fire.

American soldiers once used Tootsie Rolls to plug bullet holes during the Civil War.

Wars are always fought with lavish, maybe ridiculous, code names. During the Battle of Chosin Reservoir, U.S. troops found themselves outnumbered. They were also fighting a battle in freezing temperatures and running low on mortar shells. They radioed in for supplies, specifically mortar shells, which were codenamed "Tootsie Rolls." When the crate of ammunition arrived, it was filled with real Tootsie Roll candies. Someone had taken the codename a little too seriously. Fortunately, they could still use the candies. They warmed them and patched bullet holes in various objects. The temperatures were cold enough to make reliable, if sweet, welds.

The only living vegetation in the biggest desert in the world was hit by a drunk driver.

The most isolated acacia tree on Earth lived for approximately three centuries in the Sahara Desert. This was the only tree for 250 miles and was an important landmark for the caravans that trekked across the sands. In 1973, the Tree of Tenere was struck down. The only object in 250 miles of open desert was taken out by a drunk driver. A statue was placed where the tree once stood, and the dried-out tree trunk is on display in the Niger National Museum.

Foot powder once got elected as mayor in Ecuador.

Local elections see candidates putting signs, flyers, and stickers on any available surface. It wears out the community, and most people joke about entering a ridiculous candidate for a bit of fun. In the mayoral election for Picoaza, Ecuador, in 1967, the joke was taken a step further. One of the candidates was just a marketing ploy. *Pulvapies* foot powder put up marketing flyers everywhere using a "Vote for Pulvapies" slogan. Pamphlets were even sent to voters telling them to vote for *Pulvapies*. The foot powder won the mayoral election by a landslide.

Scotsmen may be shot with a bow and arrow in York, except on Sundays.

One of England's bizarre ancient laws, that remains part of their statutes to this day, is the permission to shoot any Scotsman with a bow and arrow upon sight, six days of the week. If a Scotsman is seen on a Sunday carrying a weapon or being intoxicated, he can still be killed, just not with a bow and arrow.

Sunglasses were first worn by Chinese judges in the 12th century to hide their emotions.

Today, sunglasses are only fashion accessories that shield our eyes from harsh sunlight. In the 12th century, however, Chinese judges wore glasses made from smoky quartz to hide their emotions from the witnesses they were questioning.

The shortest war in history lasted only 38 minutes.

In 1896, a new sultan took over in Zanzibar, which was a British colony at the time. The new ruler did not have the approval of the English, but Sultan Khalid bin Barghash stuck to his point. The Brits promptly sent warships to bombard the palace. It only took 38 minutes before the sultan fled, though.

Spanish sport stars don't sing along with their national anthem because the music has no words.

Spanish players at the 2018 Soccer World Cup found themselves in a Twitterstorm because the players looked like they refused to sing their own national anthem. The truth of the matter is that the anthem, the "Marcha Real," was composed in 1761 by Manuel de Espinosa de los Monteros as a military march. Although some people tried writing lyrics through the years, the Spanish government has not approved any of the attempts.

Cheese-Rolling is an official English sport.

For the last 200 years, participants have gathered every year at Cooper's Hill near Gloucester, England, on the Spring Bank Holiday, to chase the cheese. A judge rolls a 7–9 pound round of Double Gloucester cheese down the 200-yard hill and competitors race each other after it. The first one over the finish line gets the cheese. The rolling cheese is seldom caught physically because it can reach speeds up to 70 miles per hour.

London's black cabs had to be tall enough to accommodate a bowler hat.

The iconic tall, black cabs roaming London's streets were first introduced in the 17th century. In those years, all gentlemen wore tall bowler hats when they left their houses and the cabs' roofs had to be high enough for them to fit in comfortably. Although fashion has changed since, the custom was retained.

The longest name of a place on earth contains 85 letters.

Are you ready to get your tongue around 'Taumatawhakatangihangako-

auauotamateaturipukakapik-

imaungahoronukupokaiwhen-

uakitanatahu?"

It is a hill in New Zealand that was named after a local legendary warrior, Taumata.

The longest URL contains the second longest place name in the world.

The Welsh village of:

"Llanfairpwllgwyngyllgogerychwyrnd-

robwllllantysiliogogogoch"

on the island of Ynys Môn (the Isle of Anglesey) claims to have the longest address (URL) in the world for its official website:

"lanfairpwllgwyngyllgogerychwyrndrobwllllantysiliogogogoc h.co.uk" does seem a fair contender for the title!

Old Persian cuneiform script was first deciphered because of a bet.

Georg Friedrich Grotefend (June 9, 1775–December 15, 1853) became known for laying the foundation for deciphering old Persian documents written in cuneiform. His success came by chance, though. One of his friends believed it would be impossible to read a language about which nothing is known; Grotefend didn't agree and made a bet with the friend that he could figure out a cuneiform script.

The world's oldest hotel was founded in 705.

Japan's Nisiyama Onsen Keiunkan hotel opened its doors in Yamanashi in the year 705. It is situated at a hot spring and still operates as a working establishment, ready to receive visitors.

The Milanese are legally obliged to smile at all times.

According to a law made in the 19th century that has never been repealed, residents of the Italian city of Milan have to smile whenever they are in public. The only exceptions to the rule are during hospital visits or funerals.

Pigeon poo is royal property in England.

The British royals own many fabulous objects that ordinary people covet. Although bird droppings do not, unfortunately, fall into this category, they are the property of the British crown. In the 18th century, the droppings were used as an ingredient in gunpowder, so King George I claimed all of it—even sending guards to watch over some of the pigeons.

You could mail your kid to grandma in the beginning of the 20th century.

Between 1913 and 1915, seven people took advantage of the vague rules of the U.S. postal service in the early years of the package service. Parcels over four pounds were accepted, but there were no clear guidelines as to the contents. Classifying the children as "harmless live animals," kids with the required number of postage stamps in their pockets were handed to the mailman and put on trains to go visit grandma.

The highest number of wickets taken by one player in first class cricket is more than 4,000.

Wilfred Rhodes, who played 58 test matches for England between 1899 and 1930, took 4,204 wickets during his career. Just to sweeten the tidbit even further for cricket enthusiasts, he also scored a total of 39, 969 runs.

American President Andrew Jackson's pet parrot swore so much during his owner's funeral that it had to be removed from the scene.

The seventh president of the United States, Andrew Jackson, who was in power from 1829 to 1837, had an African Grey parrot named Poll that picked up a habit of swearing. After Jackson's death on June 8, 1845, a big group of mourners gathered at his home for the funeral. The crowd excited the bird and he commenced swearing loudly. It upset the people so much that the bird had to be taken away.

May 29th is officially "Put a Pillow on Your Fridge" Day in both the United States and Europe.

This day evolved from an earlier tradition to put a cloth in the larder once a year to bring good luck. Larders were used for cold storage before electric fridges became common. The pillow can either be put on top of the fridge or literally crammed inside for the day, in the hope of improving prosperity and bringing good fortune.

In 1633, drinking coffee in public in Turkey could have cost you your life.

Turkey was ruled by the brutal Sultan Murad IV of the Ottoman Empire from 1623 to 1640. During his reign, he beheaded anyone that was seen drinking coffee because he regarded the beverage as a narcotic substance. He also prohibited coffee shops because he believed they would encourage conversations against his rulership.

The Egyptian pharaoh Pepi II smeared slaves with honey to keep flies away from himself.

Pharaoh Pepi II, who ruled Egypt from about 2278 B.C.E. for a period of 64 years, despised flies. To keep the insects away, he always kept naked slaves smeared with honey close to him. The flies were drawn to the honey, leaving the pharaoh alone.

The use of forks was once considered sacrilegious.

Today, we take forks for granted when setting a table, but in the West it was regarded as blasphemous to eat with a fork until the 11th century. The general belief was that forks were like artificial hands, making their use an offense to God who created us with hands to be utilized as natural forks.

Early golf balls had centers filled with honey.

Before solid core golf balls became common in the 1960s, ball manufacturers used liquid centers to help keep the ball stable during flight. Honey was popular because it never spoiled and adhered well to the outer covering of the ball. Talk about hitting a sweet shot!

Residents of one Georgia town in the US will never know why the chicken crossed the road, because the chicken is not allowed to do that.

The town of Quitman, located in the southwest of Georgia and close to the Florida border, has a law forbidding chickens to cross the road. The origins of the legislation are unknown, but it could very well have been penned by an official who got tired of hearing that particular joke.

The first speeding fine was issued for driving a reckless 8 mph.

UK resident Walter Arnold received the first speeding fine ever recorded on January 28, 1896. Not only did he exceed the speed limit four times by driving at 8 mph, but he was also charged with driving a locomotive without a horse on a public road, allowing operation of the locomotive by fewer than three people, and failing to display his name and address on the locomotive.

A leaking milk truck inspired the lining of roads down the center.

In 1911, Edward Hines—who was, at the time, the chairman of the Wayne County Board of Roads in Michigan—drove behind a truck that was dripping milk. That gave him the idea of painting lines down the middle of roadways to promote safety.

Playing the bagpipes saved the life of a Scottish soldier on D-Day during WWII.

On June 6, 1944, the Allied forces landed on five beaches in Normandy, simultaneously, to begin their assault on Hitler's stronghold in Europe. On one of the beaches, Sword, a young Scottish officer, began playing his bagpipes to keep his comrades' spirits up. He survived the day without a scratch. When later asked why he wasn't shot at, two captive German snipers said, "We thought he was merely a fool!"

Canadians needed an "Apology Act" to stop them from incriminating themselves in court.

Canadians are very polite—so polite, in fact, that they say "sorry" more than any other people. To avoid having mere polite apologies used as admissions of guilt in court cases, the "Apology Act" was adopted in 2009. The definitions in the act make it clear that the word "sorry" has to be regarded as an expression of regret or sympathy, and not as the acceptance of any criminal liability.

An undergraduate architecture student saved a Manhattan skyscraper from possible collapse.

The Citicorp Center (now known as 601 Lexington) that was built in 1977 features uniquely designed stilts at the bottom to accommodate St. Peter's Lutheran Church, situated on one corner of the property. Princeton University student Diane Hartley, later that year, researched the building for her thesis and realized that strong winds striking the building at its corners could knock it over. She phoned the architect's office and they, after checking her calculations, hastily executed emergency repairs on the building.

Male doctors invented a condition called "bicycle face" in the late 1890s to dissuade women from riding bikes.

In the 1890s, riding a bicycle was regarded as an expression of feminism in Europe and America. In an attempt to curb the growing movement toward independence for women, doctors began cautioning cyclists against the likelihood of permanent damage to a face that showed the strain of riding: flushing, drawn lips, dark shadows under the eyes, and weariness.

The staircases in medieval castles were built clockwise to protect the castle residents.

Most knights wielded their swords in their right hands. When invading soldiers were going up the stairs, they would have to round each curve before being able to attack anyone. Their swing would also be inhibited by the inner wall. The defenders, on the other hand, would have been at an advantage coming down the stairs to meet the invaders.

The Egyptian queen Cleopatra lived closer to the time when Pizza Hut was founded than to the building of the Egyptian pyramids at Giza.

Queen Cleopatra ascended the Egyptian throne in 51 B.C.E. and reigned until her death in 30 B.C.E. That puts her 2,400 years away from the building of the pyramids at Giza in around 2500 B.C.E. The first Pizza Hut started doing business in 1958, meaning there's only a gap of 2,000 years between that event and Cleopatra.

Until 2015, there was an Indian enclave, inside a Bangladeshi enclave, inside another Indian enclave, inside Bangladesh.

The little third-order enclave of Dahala Khagrabari was the only one of its type in the world. It measured two acres and was owned by a Bangladeshi jute farmer. Every morning, the farmer woke up in Bangladesh, walked over into India to work on his farm, and returned home to Bangladesh at night.

In 1978, a man ate a whole Cessna 150 airplane.

Michel Lotito was born in France in 1950, with an extraordinary thick stomach lining and a peculiar digestive system. That, combined with his desire to eat strange and dangerous objects (a condition known as *pica*), made it possible for him to devour an entire Cessna plane in two years. Besides the Cessna, he is also recorded as having digested eighteen bicycles, fifteen supermarket trolleys, seven TV sets, a computer, two beds, a pair of skis, a coffin (handles and all), and six chandeliers during his lifetime.

One ancient Egyptian mummy has a modern passport.

Egyptian Pharaoh Ramses II died in 1213 B.C.E. To foil graverobbers, his priests frequently moved his body to new locations. That caused considerable damage to the condition of the mummy and, in the 1970s, Ramses II was sent to France for some expert attention. The Egyptians, however, worried that the mummy might be kept in Europe, so they issued Ramses II a modern Egyptian passport stating his occupation as "King, deceased."

One Italian war was fought over a wooden bucket.

Although the 1325 war had only one battle that lasted two hours, it was nevertheless fiercely fought between the residents of Modena and the people living in Bologna. The war outside the town of Zappolino started when the imperial faction in Modena stole the wooden bucket outside the municipal well in Bologna, where the papal faction dominated. The fight ended in a standoff. To this day, the offending bucket is on display in Modena's municipal complex.

Iran once arrested 14 squirrels on charges of espionage.

In 2007, Iranian soldiers found 14 squirrels in the vicinity of a nuclear enrichment plant. Intelligence operatives claimed the rodents were carrying sophisticated Western spy gear. The "spies" were promptly arrested and the official report was that the enemy was successfully apprehended before any damage could be done.

The Australian army lost a war against emu birds in 1932.

In 1915, the Australian government launched a farming program to provide land where soldiers could settle after WWI. By 1932, several of the farmers threatened to leave because Australia's famous flightless birds, the emus, were eating their crops. Soldiers armed with machine guns subsequently started the emu war, as it became known, in November 1932. After 38 days of futile battle, the army conceded defeat to the birds—they were simply too quick and tough for the army.

A tornado once saved Washington DC from destruction by war.

During the oppressively hot night of August 24, 1814, British troops attacked Washington DC. They set fire to big parts of the city, continuing the next day, without taking notice of the thunder and lightning of the huge storm that was building up around them. A tornado soon formed and moved straight toward the British troops on Capitol Hill. After two hours of heavy rainfall that doused the flames, much structural damage, and the loss of several soldiers' lives, the invaders abandoned the occupation that lasted only 26 hours.

The world's smallest country measures only 15 by 40 yards.

The self-proclaimed micronation called Sealand lives on a WWII-era anti-aircraft platform in the sea off the coast of Suffolk, England. It has only one small building and a helicopter landing pad. The principality of Sealand was declared on September 2, 1967, by the former British Army Major Paddy Roy Bates, who had started the pirate radio station Radio Essex there a few months earlier.

The British national anthem was played 17 times in a row in 1909, to give King Edward VII time to struggle into his German field marshal uniform.

On February 9, 1909, King Edward VII arrived at the Rathenau railway station in Brandenburg, Germany, on a state visit. Getting dressed in his German Field-Marshal uniform before disembarking from the train proved, however, to be a problem. The German military band had to keep on playing "God save the King" until the king was ready.

The shortest national anthem has only four lines.

The Japanese national anthem called "Kimigayo" has only four lines and thirty-two characters. It is one of the oldest anthems in the world and is most likely based on a Japanese waka poem dating from the Heian period (794–1185).

Crime is illegal in Texas, unless you give 24-hour notice beforehand.

A peculiar law that is still on the books in Texas in the US makes it illegal to commit a crime without notifying the intended victim 24 hours before. The notice also needs to state the nature of the crimes to be committed.

Germans in the Middle Ages kissed a donkey to relieve toothache.

Although the origins of this dentistry advice is not known, it seems to have been widely believed. One suggestion for the reason the habit started is that the kissing was done in the hope that the donkey would kick the kisser, thereby removing the source of the pain!

Bangkok's full Thai name consists of 21 separate words.

The full Thai name is more a description than just a name. "Krung Thep Mahanakhon Amon Rattanakosin Mahinthara Ayuthaya Mahadilok Phop Noppharat Ratchathani Burirom Udomratchaniwet Mahasathan Amon Piman Awatan Sathit Sakkathattiya Witsanukam Prasit" comes from the Sanskrit and Pali languages. Roughly translated, it means, "City of angels, great city of immortals, magnificent city of the nine gems, seat of the king, city of royal palaces, home of gods incarnate, erected by Vishvakarman at Indra's behest."

Pheasant Island swaps nationalities every six months.

The 656-foot-long strip of land is located between France and Spain on the Bidasoa river. It became important after the Thirty Years War, a religious conflict that raged between France and Spain. The island was chosen as a neutral spot to demarcate the borders of the two countries. To demonstrate their goodwill toward each other, France and Spain decided to swap ownership of Pheasant Island every six months.

America's narrowest house is only seven feet wide.

Known as the Hollensbury Spite House, the skinny structure sandwiched between two bigger houses was erected in 1830 in Old Town, Virginia, by John Hollensbury. He owned one of the adjacent big homes. He got so tired of the carriage noises and loiterers in the alley between his home and the neighbor that he built a house in it. The house measures 7 feet wide, 25 feet deep, and encloses a total surface area of 325 square feet.

The first female cricketer to take 10 wickets in an innings was only 15 years old at the time.

Emma Liddell was a 15-year-old schoolgirl in Australia when she played in a cricket championship match between Metropolitan West and Metropolitan East in 1996. She showed her opponents no mercy, and her figures were 10-0 from 7.4 overs. It is exceptionally rare for cricketers to accomplish this. Liddell was only the 24th out of 25 cricketers ever to have succeeded at taking all 10 wickets in one innings, and the first woman to do so.

Nepal is the only country in the world with an asymmetrical, non-rectangular flag.

The Nepalese have a unique flag that is a combination of two single triangular shapes. The design is centuries old. The background is red with a blue border. The upper segment shows a white moon with a crescent below it, while the lower part features a white, stylized sun.

The man who had the longest beard on record was killed by his own beard.

The 16th century mayor of the German town Braunau am Inn, Hans Steininger, had a flowing beard more than four-and-a-half-feet long. He usually kept the beard neatly rolled up and tucked into one of his pockets. In 1567, a fire broke out in the town, and in the commotion he was running around with it hanging free. Unfortunately for Steininger, he stepped on his beard and tripped himself. He tumbled down a flight of stairs and broke his neck.

One Kentucky, US family had blue skin for generations.

Martin Fugate immigrated from France to the US in 1820 and settled in Troublesome Creek, Kentucky. He carried the gene for a rare skin condition called methemoglobinemia and chose the isolated, small town to stay away from other people, as far as possible. He eventually got married to a local woman who, unbelievably, also carried the gene. Because of the isolation, most of their seven children married close relatives, and the blue skin showed up in the Fugate clan for 150 years.

A small typing error cost Italian airline Alitalia $7.72 million in 2006.

At the time, the price for a ticket between Toronto, Canada and Cyprus was $3,900. An assistant made a typing error while entering the information on the airline's booking system, listing the ticket price as only $39. By the time the mistake was discovered, 509 people had already purchased tickets at the low price. In the end, Alitalia had to let around 2,000 people fly at the huge discount.

Braille was not originally intended for the blind.

A French military veteran invented a raised-dot writing system in the early 1800s to enable Napoleon's armies to read in the dark. It did not work as well as he wanted because he used 12 dots per cell, which were too many to read with only one touch. A blind boy, Louis Braille, modified the system to six dots per cell and blind people started using it.

Germany managed to lose a whole Sri Lankan national handball team in 2004.

The Asian-German Sports Exchange Programme with offices in Sri Lanka and Germany, presented a handball tournament in 2004 in Bavaria, Germany. The Sri Lankan national team of sixteen players and eight trainers vanished, however, just a few days after their arrival. German investigations later discovered that the so-called players were just ordinary citizens looking for a better life, who cleverly duped all the authorities involved. To this day, the missing Sri Lankans have not been located.

One neon light shone continuously for 77 years, racking up a bill of about $17,000.

When the new owner of a restaurant in Los Angeles started tearing down walls for renovations in 2012, he noticed a glow behind one wall. Upon investigation, he discovered a lit neon tube. It had most likely been in use since 1935, when the establishment had forest-themed murals that used neon backlighting. One of the murals was walled over in 1949, but everyone apparently forgot to disconnect the light.

The longest war in history lasted 335 years because the Dutch forgot about it.

The war took place between the Netherlands and the English islands of Scilly. It started in 1651 during the English Civil War and lasted until 1986. There were no casualties in the war and the Dutch ships sailed home after three months, forgetting to sign a peace treaty.

A Paris orphanage once held a raffle with live babies as the prizes.

In 1911, there was an alarming number of abandoned children in Paris. There was almost no legislation about child safety, and in an effort to find safe homes for the children in their care, the orphanage organized the "Loterie de Bébés."

Iceland has the oldest legislature in the world.

The Althing was founded in 930. It existed until 1798 at Thingvellir, in southwestern Iceland, when a Danish decree abolished it after the country came under Danish royal rule. The Althing was reconvened in 1845 in Reykjavik.

Oxford University is older than the Aztec civilization.

The world famous English university opened its doors to students in 1096. The Aztecs of central Mexico, in contrast, only date from 1325, when they founded the city of Tenochtitlán.

Tablecloths were originally intended as communal napkins.

In the 15th century, dinner guests did not have individual napkins. A big cloth was draped over the edge of the table, instead, on which they could wipe their hands and mouths.

The heaviest baby ever born weighed 22 pounds.

The baby was born on January 19, 1879, to exceptionally tall parents, who were designated as the tallest couple ever by the Guinness Book of World Records. Anna Bates (née Swan) measured seven feet and eleven inches. Her husband, Martin van Buren Bates, stood seven feet and nine inches tall. The baby (twenty-eight inches in length) unfortunately only lived eleven hours.

The Romans once had a horse as a senator.

Roman emperor Caligula, also known as Gaius, had a horse he loved so much that he made him a senator. Incitatus had his own marble stall in a manger made from ivory, and he wore a jeweled collar. It is alleged that Caligula planned to make his beloved horse a consul before he was assassinated.

Hamburgers were known as "liberty steaks" in the US for a short while.

During WWII, the Americans felt that the name "hamburger" sounded too German. They renamed it "liberty steak," but the most facetious moniker was dropped after the war.

The fastest surgeon in history also once had a 300 % mortality rate.

Before anesthesia came into regular use, surgeons tried to perform any operations as fast as possible to minimize a patient's pain. Dr. Robert Liston was famous for being one of the fastest, particularly with amputations. He once amputated a patient's leg so quickly that he accidentally cut his assistant's fingers off, too. Both the patient and the assistant died afterward of blood poisoning, while one spectator died from a heart attack.

The longest recorded year had 445 days.

Nicknamed the "year of confusion," the year 46 B.C.E. lasted 445 days after Julius Caesar added 3 months to it. He planned to introduce a reformed calendar system the next year and needed to match the old, seasonal Roman calendar to the new model.

A medieval town constructed inside a meteor crater is made of diamonds.

The small south-German town of Nördlingen was built 1,110 years ago inside a depression the founders of the town thought was formed through volcanic activity. The site turned out to be 15 million years old and made up entirely of microscopic diamonds. The precious stones formed during the incredible pressure the asteroid's impact exerted on the rock.

The longest overdue library book was returned after 288 years.

Col. Robert Walpole borrowed a book on the Archbishop of Bremen in 1667–68 from the library of Sidney Sussex College in Cambridge, England. During one of his research trips 288 years later, the British historian Prof. Sir John Plumb found the book in the library of the Marquess of Cholmondeley in Norfolk. Though he dutifully returned the book to the college in 1956, they declined to exact a fine.

CHaPTer 2: INVenTors and INVenTIons

A scathing obituary of the still-alive Alfred Nobel led to the creation of the Nobel Prize.

You probably didn't know that the esteemed Nobel Prize started with an obituary for a man who wasn't dead. A newspaper ran Alfred Nobel's obituary, probably because of mistaken information. They boldly used the headline "The merchant of death is dead." This referred to Nobel's invention of dynamite and the number of lives dynamite had claimed. This irked the Swedish engineer. He decided to leave his whole fortune to the Nobel Prize Institution to recognize people across the world for the benefit they bring to mankind.

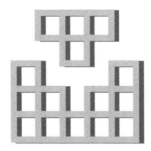

The inventor of Tetris never got to reap the rewards.

Anyone who plays video games has probably tried "Tetris" once or twice. It was wildly popular some years ago. Alexey Pajitnov invented the game in 1984, but because he lived in the Soviet Union, he had to give up all his rights as creator to the government. He eventually received some royalties in the 1990s, but he didn't get to capitalize on the iconic music. The music used in the game is in the public domain, so anyone can use it without having to pay.

The Serbian-American inventor, electrical engineer, mechanical engineer, and futurist Nikola Tesla once fell in love with a pigeon.

Nikola Tesla was brilliant, and he is best known for his work in electric power. While he had several patents, he also had an eccentric side that annoyed many people who were around him. One particular quirk was his love of pigeons. He often spent much time feeding pigeons in the park, and he left his window open for pigeons to come into his room. His room was often in disarray, thanks to the birds. One particular pigeon caught the romantic eye of the inventor. He said he loved the pigeon the way a man loves a woman. Moreover, he believed the pigeon loved him back.

The guillotine was invented to provide equality in French punishment.

If we think of the guillotine, what is the first thing that comes to mind? Usually, it is France or the French Revolution. While we regard this form of punishment as barbaric now, it was—at the time—a more civilized approach compared to the methods used before. However, the principle behind the invention is the most remarkable. The guillotine was brought in by the equality movement that was sweeping France during the revolution to ensure that, from peasants to royalty, the death sentence was carried out in an equal manner for all.

The man who invented FM radio was the victim of corporate bullying.

Edwin Armstrong created the idea for FM radio in 1933. He had several innovations for radio to his credit, but he was bullied by big corporations and stripped of his patents by the government. He believed FM radio was going to change his luck and his fortune. The radio industry was, however, not keen on change despite the rave reviews of the people who picked up the early broadcasts. The industrial moguls hated to share wealth with someone else and got the courts to change the frequencies. That made Armstrong's receivers obsolete. He took his own life after losing the court cases, his wife, and all of his money. He died believing that FM radio had failed and never saw its success.

Early inventor James A. Williams made a mousetrap that was a revolver.

In 1882, James A. Williams invented a deadly mousetrap that was actually a .50 caliber revolver. He took his inspiration from 19th century so-called burglar alarms that rigged weapons with a lever mechanism to kill anyone opening the door or window where the "alarm" was installed. The invention never really took off because people were wary of keeping a spring-loaded weapon under the kitchen counter.

In the 1800s, a *mass* shaving machine was invented.

During the 19th century, men preferred getting their shaves at a barber shop. To speed things up a bit, a shaving machine that boasted shaving at least a dozen men at once was invented in England. It turned out to be a commercial failure, though. The biggest flaw of the machine was that it could not alter its movements to accommodate different face shapes. Shave and a face cut, anyone?

Microwave ovens were invented totally by accident.

The modern household changed when the microwave hit the market. You can probably still find old cookbooks that rely solely on the appliance. However, this time-saving device didn't evolve after years of research just to benefit households. In 1946, Percy Spencer was working with radar when he noticed that a piece of candy in his pocket had melted. He experimented with other foods, and the results were the same, every time. That means minor accidents led to the creation of the microwave.

Bubble wrap started life as wallpaper.

Alfred Fielding and Marc Shuvon were engineers set on creating a textured wallpaper—not just any textured wallpapers, but a 3D one, at that. Their material of choice was plastic, and they produced a bubbly plastic sheet. Sadly, no one was interested in their innovative wallpaper. To save the day, they formed the Sealed Air Corporation and started marketing the failed wallpaper as a new way to package fragile objects for safe shipping. Who knew they'd also give us hours of entertainment, years later still, when we pop all those little bubbles?

Henry Ford built a successful flying car.

Ford had much success in getting almost every U.S. citizen to buy a car, but he didn't stop there. He wanted to give people easy access to planes, as well. Work on the Ford Flivver began in 1926.

The flaps were designed to allow the craft to take off in small spaces, and the rear wheel would make it possible for the pilot to drive from their home to a runway. The first Flivver took to the skies in 1928. Pilot Harry J. Brooks flew from Michigan to Miami on one tank of gas. However, when Brooks was over the ocean, the plane's engine seized up, leading to a tragic accident. Ford scrapped the project.

LaMarcus Thompson invented roller coasters to keep people from sin.

In the 1880s, businessman LaMarcus Thompson hated how Amercians were tempted by less desirable places like saloons and brothels. As a means of "cleaning up" what he considered to be one of the most immoral places on earth, he built the first roller coaster in Coney Island, New York, as a way to distract the public from their hedonistic pastimes.

Inventor John Rose took his frameless glasses a pinch far.

In 2004, the American inventor John Rose decided to improve on the *pince-nez,* frameless glasses that pinched the wearer's nose to stay put. He registered a patent for a pair of glasses with studs that pierced the person's nose. Alternatively, if the wearer preferred eyebrow studs, the glasses could be fitted to those, too. Nobody knows how many pairs of these glasses, straight from a horror movie, were sold; but, the inventor's website has disappeared since.

Stop and smell the cacti with a greenhouse helmet.

Have you always wanted your own personal biosphere? The greenhouse helmet, invented by the American Waldemar Anguita in 1986, provided just that. It consisted of a dome that fitted over a person's head and neck, resting on the shoulders. Inside the dome, tiny cacti and other small plants arranged close to the person's ears gave off oxygen for the helmet wearer to breathe.

Solve your storage problems with floating furniture.

An enterprising Chinese inventor registered a patent in 1989 for furniture that could float to the ceiling on helium. The body of the furniture was made from a rubber-like fabric that could be inflated with helium gas. When tidying up in the morning, the bed and other pieces of furniture could simply be stored against the ceiling. At night, it could be pulled down again with a tether rope.

The ultimate snack accessory is a motorized ice-cream cone.

If you love ice cream, you'll know how easy it is to end up with sticky drops of ice cream on your hands and clothes. Enter the motorized ice-cream cone, invented in 1999 by Richard B. Hartman. For less than $10, you can still get your hands on a colorful plastic cone that spins at the touch of a button, to ensure your sweet treat gets licked evenly. The inventor even envisaged making icy sculptures and patterns with the tongue!

Never lose your watch again with a subdermal model.

A sure way to have the time of day (or night) when you need it is to get your watch implanted under your skin. A U.S. patent was issued in 1997 for a watch with LED lights that can be implanted just below the skin of the arm. Skin is translucent, so it will be easy to read the digits, according to the inventor. The remote control for the watch also allows the display to be changed to a custom message, creating a subdermal tattoo.

The invention of the tea bag resulted from a misunderstanding.

A New York tea merchant named Thomas Sullivan sent samples of his tea to some of his customers in 1908. The tea leaves were contained in small silken bags. The customers didn't understand they had to remove the leaves from the bags, and used them as they were. After receiving lots of positive feedback after the misunderstanding, Sullivan began marketing proper tea bags.

The chain saw was invented to be used as a surgical instrument in hospitals.

While your first association with a chain saw may be a horror movie, the invention was actually intended to save lives. Two Scottish doctors (working independently from each other) conceived the idea in the late 18th century to, respectively, assist in childbirth and remove diseased bone.

The toothbrush was invented in 1498 by a Chinese emperor.

Emperor Hongzhi of the Ming Dynasty in China wanted to clean his teeth better than was possible up to that time. People used to chew on sticks, using the frayed ends to clean between their teeth, or they simply wiped their teeth with a cloth. Hongzhi stuck some of the coarse, hard hair from a hog's back into a bamboo stick, and the toothbrush was born.

ARE YOU ENJOYING MY BOOK?

At the risk of interrupting your reading experience and potentially coming across as a bit of a bother (*which I truly do hope I am not*), I would love to know if you are enjoying the read so far? If so, this is fabulous news! A great deal of work goes into anything I produce, and as a full-time author, reviews are the foundation of my livelihood. I rely on them as a "green light" for other readers who may consider giving mine a whirl. So, to aid in my quest for more "book whirling," I hope you might review this one.

If so, I will take it as a virtual "high five!" And to make the process easier, I have listed the direct review links below.

U.S: https://bit.ly/BTB_US

U.K: https://bit.ly/BTB_UK

Canada: https://bit.ly/BTB_CA

Australia: https://bit.ly/BTB_AU

CHAPTER 3: POP CULTURE

One scene in *The Terminator* seemed so realistic because it was.

There was one scene in the first *Terminator* movie where the Terminator punches a hole through a car window to hotwire the vehicle. Normally, these scenes are shot with windows that are made of melted sugar, with the sound effects added later. When filming started, they found out there was no permit to film on that particular street where their "set car" was parked. Director James Cameron needed the shot urgently and simply told his lead actor, Arnold Schwarzenegger, to cross the street on which they were and punch the window of one of the parked cars out. Not only was the window made of real glass, but the car did not even belong to the movie set. When the police arrived, the crew had some explaining to do!

Music can make us more generous.

This was tested in a study done in Japan in 2014. The two scientists divided a group of 22 people into a "dictator" group and a "recipient" group. The dictators had to hand out money to the recipients while either listening to some background music they liked, music they disliked, or during complete silence. The music was compiled according to the song choices the participants submitted to the researchers before the study. The results showed that the people who listened to the music they liked were far more generous than any of the others.

The most profitable film in history is called *Paranormal Activity*.

It seems weird after living through the ages of *Avatar, Titanic,* and a majority of Marvel movies that a horror film would be the most profitable. *Paranormal Activity* didn't gross a billion dollars at the box office, but that doesn't matter because movie profits are based on the return on investment (ROI). When you break the numbers down, the film only cost $60,000 to make and about $400,000 to market. After its release, the movie made over $89 million, which adds up to a ROI of close to 20,000%.

The mysterious code in *The Matrix* was only symbols from a cookbook.

When the first film in the series came out, people were hooked by the story and the computer generated imagery (CGI). One thing they could not figure out, though, was what the code actually meant. Turns out, it was only some symbols taken from a sushi cookbook.

The fans of heavy metal and classical music have more in common than you might think.

The worlds of heavy metal and classical music don't usually meet. The closest they ever got was probably in September 2019, when Metallica took the stage on two separate occasions with the San Francisco Symphony Orchestra. The fans of the two genres are, however, more similar than you may have thought. According to psychological data, both groups are highly creative, very gentle, and have high levels of confidence in themselves.

Boxer Gus Waldorf became famous for losing a boxing match to a bear.

For some strange reason, humans have always wanted to test their strength against bears. Whether it was boxing or wrestling, there was always someone willing to challenge these beasts. A little-known boxer by the name of Gus Waldorf decided in 1949 that an official boxing fight with a bear would be just what his career needed. The bear won the fight right after the beginning of the first round, with a mighty right that sent Waldorf sprawling. Although he lost the fight, Waldorf did, however, gain the notoriety he wanted.

Hollywood actor Sylvester Stallone ended up in the hospital during the filming of *Rocky IV* because he wanted the fighting to look authentic.

One of the main characters in *Rocky IV* is Ivan Drago. He is the Soviet Union's most-feared boxer who ends up killing Rocky's former rival-turned-friend, Apollo Creed. Rocky then fights the super-boxer and ultimately triumphs. Sylvester Stallone, who played the role of Rocky, wanted the fights to look realistic. He instructed martial artist Dolph Lundgren, who played the role of Drago, to hit him for real. That turned out to be a bad decision, because one of the punches Stallone took in the chest put him in intensive care for eight days.

Music trends correlate with the stock market.

Although music cannot directly affect the stock market, there seems to be a correlation between the price trends in the markets and the type of music that was popular during that time. Professor Alex Edmans, from the London Business School, found in his research conducted in 2021 that prices rose in the weeks when the residents of a particular country listened to happy, up-beat music. When the mood turned negative, as reflected in music choices, prices fell. Market volatility was also mirrored in music choices that jumped back and forth between extreme positivity and extreme negativity.

Japanese golfers have "hole-in-one insurance."

When we think of insurance in sport, we think of injuries to the athletes or general insurance against accidents during matches. In Japan, however, about four million golfers are insured in case they manage to get the elusive hole-in-one. The first policy was offered in 1982 and amateur players pay a premium of $65 a year for $3,500 in coverage. The reason for this? Getting a hole-in-one is a big deal, and everyone will want to share in the golfer's happiness. Having a policy that pays out $3,500 will cover the food and drinks that will become necessary after playing such a great shot.

Rower Bobby Pearce won his Olympic event despite stopping during the race.

In the 1928 Olympics, Australian Bobby Pearce took part in the rowing competition against eight other competitors. At some point during the race, he stopped to let a group of ducks pass in front of him. Despite the delay, Pearce still won the gold medal in the event.

The first drive-thru restaurant was installed to help soldiers.

Soldiers stationed at the Fort Huachuca military base in Arizona loved buying food from the McDonald's closeby; but, in the US, they were not allowed to be seen in public wearing their military uniforms. That meant they had to change into civilian clothes just to grab a bite. To help them, the owner of the restaurant knocked a hole in one of the walls so they could pick up their orders without leaving the car.

A beach town in California has a blimp as its official bird.

The Goodyear blimp is well-known and loved in the US. The town of Redondo Beach, close to the home airport of the blimp in Carson, California, passed legislation in 1983 to make the blimp the town's official bird.

Pirates of the Caribbean: On Stranger Tides, produced in 2011, is the most expensive movie ever made to date.

With its budget of $378.5 million, which was later adjusted to $422 million for inflation, the fourth movie in the *Pirates* series was the most expensive film ever as of 2022. Some of the reasons for this include the high number of shooting locations, 10 different companies involved in creating the special effects, and the expensive 3D cameras that were used.

The dating app *Tinder* once made a match in Antarctica.

One night in 2014, a lonely American scientist working at the McMurdo base station logged on to the popular matchmaking site to see if he could find a date. Not only did he find one, but she was only 45 minutes (by helicopter ride) away at a deep field camp. She was in her tent, surfing through potential matches on the mobile dating app, at the exact moment the scientist started searching for a date.

Japan has produced more than 300 different flavors of Kit Kat chocolate bars since 2000.

The Japanese have a love affair with the little chocolate bars that started with the name of the sweets. Kit Kat sounds like the Japanese words *kitto katsu* which means "you're sure to win" or "good luck." Sweet red-bean soup, pumpkin cheesecake, lemon vinegar, salt and puff, and green soybean rice cake are some of the exotic flavors available.

Wimbledon line judges have to learn swear words in many different languages.

No, swearing is not a prerequisite for being a good line judge. No swearing is allowed on Wimbledon, so the judges have to know several different swear words to be able to recognize them if a player uses any profanity on court.

A Finnish wife's weight can be worth plenty of beer to her husband.

The Fins have a sport called "wife carrying." Men have to negotiate an obstacle course while carrying their wives over their shoulders. The winner receives his wife's weight in beer.

Extreme ironing combines a love for the outdoors with having well-pressed clothes.

Taking a standard iron and ironing board to extreme locations to press a garment has gained quite a following among outdoor sports enthusiasts. Ironing while skydiving, canoeing, surfing, and bungee jumping are only a few of the activities reported.

The shortest published paper in the world contains zero words.

It was published in 1974 in the *Journal of Applied Behavior Analysis* by Dennis Upper. The subject is "The unsuccessful self-treatment of a case of 'writer's block.'"

Facial hair can steal your beer.

Beer company Guinness once estimated that as much as 93,000 liters of beer are lost in men's facial hair every year in the UK.

An American restaurant chain is an informal indication of storm severity in the US.

The Waffle House Index has been used by weather bureaus since 2011 to gauge how bad a storm is. This comes from the Waffle House's legendary preparedness to face disasters and to recover in record time if they had to close their doors due to a storm.

Snow White's seven dwarfs almost did not have the names we know today.

Disney studio considered a whole host of other names before settling on the ones we know them by. The possibilities included Baldy, Gabby, Scrappy, Chesty, Tubby, Burpy, Deafy, Hickey, Wheezy, and Awful.

Mobile phone throwing is an official sport in Finland.

It started in 2000, when a mobile phone company wanted to help their employees to reduce their frustrations by taking it out on their phones. The people enjoyed it so much that Finland started organizing the Mobile Phone Throwing World Championships every August.

The New York town of Lily Dale is dedicated to psychics, mediums, and spiritualists.

The small town, an hour southwest of Buffalo, New York, with its charming cottages and picket fences, has only one prerequisite for its population of about 275. All of them are psychics or mediums. The town was founded in 1879 as a summer retreat for the religion of Spiritualism, whose followers believe the deceased still interact with the living.

There is a real movie about paint drying.

A young British filmmaker, Charlie Lyne, wanted to show his unhappiness with the mandatory and costly classification and rating system for all British movies by the British Board of Film Classification (BBFC). He created a 10-hour-long movie showing only a brick wall with white paint drying on it. Members of the BBFC had to sit through the entire 10 hours to rate it.

The word describing a fear for long words is one of the longest in the dictionary.

"Hippopotomonstrosesquipedaliophobia" is guaranteed to give anyone with this phobia the chills at 35 letters long. It contains the word "sesquipedalian," which means "long word"—that's why the phobia is also sometimes called "sesquipedalophobia."

You can qualify as a pirate at MIT.

The Massachusetts Institute of Technology (MIT) has made a long-standing student tradition official by deciding to award graduation certificates to any undergraduate students who qualify as pirates. To finish successfully, candidates have to pass courses in archery, fencing, sailing, and pistol shooting.

A Colorado man holds the world record for pushing a peanut up Pikes Peak with his nose.

Needing only seven days to trek up the 14,115 foot Pikes Peak, Bob Salem completed the distance of 12.6 miles in a new record time. Salem is only the fourth person to attempt pushing a peanut up the mountain with his nose, and the first one in the 21st century. The previous world record of six days was set in 1963 by Ulysses Baxter.

The lifespan of pop musicians is 25 years shorter, on average, than the rest of the adult population.

The mental, emotional, and physical toll exacted by today's pop music scene on the artists is brutal. In a study undertaken in Sydney in 2014, researchers found pop musicians had accidental death rates that were between five and ten times greater, their suicide rates were between two and seven times greater, and their chances of dying in a homicide were up to eight times greater than other people.

The longest song title has 26 words.

U.S. songwriter, actor, and singer Hoagy Carmichael wrote a song in 1943 he called, "I'm a cranky old Yank in a clanky old tank on the streets of Yokohama with my Honolulu mama doin' those beat-o, beat-o flat-on-my-seat-o, Hirohito blues." Carmichael later claimed the title should have ended after "Yank" and the rest was added only as a joke.

The longest piano piece ever takes 18 hours 40 minutes to perform.

Composer Erik Satie created his "Vexations" in 1893. It consists of only 180 notes, but the composer left instructions that the theme should be repeated 840 times. During the first public performance in 1963, it was played by a relay team of 10 pianists. At the conclusion of the event, only six of the original audience members were left, with one mischievously shouting, "Encore!"

The youngest Grammy award winner was only 14 years old at the time.

The country-pop singer LeAnn Rimes won a Grammy in 1997, at age 14, for her recording of the song "Blue." She was recognized as the best female country vocal performer and the best new artist of that year.

Competitive slapping is a sport in Russia.

The first contest in this new sport took place in March 2019. Not only does the winner have to slap someone else the hardest, but also has to endure being slapped the longest time. The first champion was Vasiliy Kamotskiy, who received almost $500 in prize money.

The largest dish in the world is a traditional Bedouin special treat.

The largest menu item ever recorded is a whole roast camel, stuffed with two lambs, stuffed with about twenty chickens, stuffed with fish, stuffed with eggs. It is sometimes called "camel turducken." (Turducken is a turkey, stuffed with a duck, stuffed with a chicken.) It takes twenty-four hours to cook this meal.

You have 177,147 different ways to tie your necktie.

Swedish mathematician Mikael Vejdemo-Johansson calculated that, if you work on the assumption that an average tie can be wound 11 times before it becomes impractically short, you have a bewildering choice of possible looks. His quest was apparently inspired by the unique tie knots in the movie "The Matrix Reloaded."

The most expensive biscuit ever sold on auction fetched $23,000.

The Spillers and Bakers Pilot cracker was taken from a lifeboat by a survivor of the Titanic disaster in April 1912. The passenger, James Fenwick, kept the biscuit in an envelope with a note that explained where it came from. The snack was put up for auction in 2015 and a Greek collector of Titanic memorabilia paid £15,000 ($23,000) for it.

Mary really had a little lamb.

In the early 1800s, an 11 year-old girl from Boston named Mary Sawyer had a pet lamb that one day followed her to school. The lamb was apparently sickly, and she nursed him back to life. Afterward, he walked with her everywhere she went. Whether this tale is the origin of the well-known children's rhyme is, however, still hotly debated.

Gender-based baby colors started out with pink for boys and blue for girls.

Before pastel colors came into fashion for baby clothes in the early 19th century, both genders used to be dressed in white. By 1918, the general rule promoted by department stores was that pink was a strong color, therefore better suited to boys. Blue was regarded as a delicate, feminine color. Today's preference of using the colors the other way round was only established around 1940.

Actor Daniel Radcliffe broke more than 80 wands while filming the *Harry Potter* movies.

Despite only one magical wand choosing Harry Potter in J. K. Rowling's massively popular stories, the actor who played the role of Harry went through more than 80 prop wands during filming. He explained that he liked to drum on his legs with the wands, and after three or four weeks, they would simply break because of wear and tear.

Using Apple's iTunes for building nuclear weapons is not allowed.

I'm not kidding you! One of the clauses in the Terms and Conditions of iTunes expressly states that iTunes may not be used to develop, design, manufacture, or produce nuclear, chemical, or biological weapons or missiles.

To predict a hand of cards, you would have to take more possible combinations into account than there are known stars in the universe.

The possible arrangements in a deck of 52 playing cards is estimated at:

80,658,175,170,943,878,571,660,636,856,

403,766,975,289,505,440,883,277,824,

000,000,000,000.

That is 52 factorial: which amounts to,

roughly estimated, an 8 followed by 67 zeroes.

CHAPTER 4: SCIENCE AND NATURE

Bananas are radioactive.

Bananas are nutritious, quick snacks. They also make delicious banana bread and banana pudding, but they are really radioactive. This is caused by their high potassium content. A small subgroup of potassium atoms, called K-40, is relatively unstable and they decay spontaneously. The process produces some radioactivity. The dose is so low, however, that it poses no risk to humans.

Human intervention resulted in the pollen-seeking, regular honeybee becoming a killer.

During the 1950s, when Brazilian biologists began breeding European bees with African bees to increase honey production, the killer bee was born. The aggressive hybrid bees spread into various countries, causing death to about 1,000 people to date. The creation of the killers could have been avoided if a visiting bee keeper didn't remove the enclosure screens that separated the species, allowing 26 swarms to escape into the wild.

Vanilla can be produced from plastic bottles.

With the demand for vanillin (the primary component of the vanilla bean extract) increasing every year, Scottish researchers found a way to transform plastic into vanilla flavoring. During 2021, they produced vanilla by allowing genetically engineered E. coli bacteria to consume old plastic bottles. The process has not been declared safe for human consumption yet, but the researchers are confident its safety will be proven soon.

There is a shade of black that absorbs all but 0.04% of visible light.

Vantablack is the blackest substance known on Earth. Made of carbon nanotubes, vantablack absorbs 99.965% of the radiation in the visible spectrum. Vantablack was named after Vertically Aligned NanoTube Arrays (Vanta). When light hits its surface, the light waves get trapped inside the nanotubes and they emerge as infrared light, leaving only about 0.04% of visible light.

Once upon a time there were four separate species of humans.

Humankind didn't always have only one species. German scientists carefully studied the human-like fossils found in Kenya, Ethiopia, and Chad. They concluded that four distinct species of humans all lived at the same time. It is possible they had no idea about each other's existence, because this occurred more than three million years ago.

Some of the apples sold at the market are a year old already.

Have you ever wondered how it's possible to buy fresh apples in May, while harvest time for apples is between August and November? Harvested apples that are not sold immediately are covered in wax, dried in hot air, and put into cold storage. After six to 12 months, the "fresh apples" are finally available for purchase.

Your brain is smaller than a caveman's.

It's probably all those hours of television and video games that shrunk our brains, right? Wrong. While our brains have shrunk somewhat compared to the size of human brains from 10,000 years ago, ancient humans were always in survival mode. Their brains had to be larger than ours to ensure their survival. Where we live, however, is also relevant. Research done in 2019 on eight Antarctica dwellers before they left for the area, and again 14 months later when they returned, showed that the isolation and monotony shrunk their brains even more.

Your leg is strong enough to break concrete.

You shouldn't try to put your leg against concrete in a bar bet, but it is useful to know that your femur is four times stronger than concrete. The thigh is the strongest, largest, and densest bone in the body. A femur can withstand tremendous pressure and it could be used as a dangerous weapon.

The "thinner you" you're looking for just lives in another part of the world.

The strength of the gravitational pull on earth varies because our planet is not a perfect sphere. The Hudson Bay in Canada, for example, has far less gravity than other places because an ice sheet dented the planet more than 10,000 years ago. When you visit these places, check your weight and not your mass, and you'll be pleasantly surprised with the results.

Earth is recycling itself.

Though the ground we stand on feels permanent, it is not true. The earth goes through a regeneration process around every 500 million years. Tectonic plates bump into each other and that causes the oceanic crust to slide in under the continental crust. That movement, in turn, sets the scene for volcanic eruptions that will create a new landscape.

Only two things are hardwired into our brains to really scare us.

Most of us have phobias; some of us hate snakes or spiders, while others have a fear of the dark. These things, however, are not wired into our brains. According to scientists, we are born fearing only falling and loud sounds. All the other fears are learned, and our brains process them through the cortical processes of reasoning. Falling and loud sounds, on the other hand, activate our instinctive fight-or-flight response, and we don't stop to think first before we get scared.

It's possible you saw the Big Bang on television years ago.

This is even predating the American sitcom that began in 2007, and far predating the invention of digital TV sets. Unless you were lucky enough to have cable TV, there were only three or four channels to watch. That left many channels showing only black and white static. A tiny percentage of the static was probably the afterglow of the Big Bang.

Some stars have a giant diamond at their cores.

The first star that could have been "a girl's best friend" was discovered in the Centaurus constellation in 2004. Scientists found the white dwarf BPM 37093 to be an incredibly dense star—so dense that it has the same mass as the sun, although it is only a third of the size of Earth. They were further amazed to find that the carbon core of the star had cooled and crystallized into a massive diamond of around 10 billion trillion trillion carats. The star was nicknamed "Lucy" after the Beatles' song. Other "Lucys" have been found since the original discovery.

Gamma-ray explosions will give us radiation poisoning if they reach us.

Gamma-ray explosions are the strongest type of explosion possible in the known universe, occurring when a star turns into a supernova. The explosions cause immense amounts of electromagnetic radiation. Supernovas form all the time without harming us, but WR104 might be a bit different. It is about 7,800 light years away from us. WR104 is the other half of a binary pair of stars that spin so fast that the stellar winds are incredibly strong. If a very specific chain of events is in place when WR104 goes supernova, the gamma rays could be pointed at us. It is very unlikely that this will happen, but you never know...

There is a "zombie" star that just won't die.

Another rare supernova event was discovered in 2014. When astronomers found a supernova fading away, they thought they had been too late and had only captured the end of its cycle. Then the dying star rose from the dead, so to speak, and started shining brighter again. It seems the supernova was refueling and exploding again. The fact that a supernova had been recorded in the same spot almost 60 years before supported the theory. A possible reason for this phenomenon could be that the star is more massive than believed before, and it's holding off a supernova by continuously shedding material.

The sunsets on Mars appear blue.

Earth is not the only planet that experiences beautiful sunsets. A sunset on Mars will appear blue to anyone witnessing the event while on the red planet. During the day, Mars shows its familiar rust color. As nightfall approaches, the fine dust closer to the sun will cause the Martian sky to turn blue.

The longest visible rainbow lasted almost nine hours.

Rainbows usually last only for a few minutes, but there is one on record in Taiwan that stayed visible for 8 hours and 58 minutes on November 30, 2017. This shattered the previous world record set in 1994 in Yorkshire, England by more than 2 hours.

Water can trap laser beams.

If you point a laser beam at running water, the light will remain inside the water until the water is turned off. Water particles are heavier than light and they slow the laser down enough to trap it, even when the flow of water is slowed down.

Peanut oil can be used to make dynamite.

Peanut oil can be processed to produce glycerol, which can be used to make nitroglycerine. The latter is a key component of dynamite. Although the peanut oil can be substituted for other processes, it shows there is truth to the explosive side of the popular little nuts' character.

A carrot saved one woman's wedding ring.

A Swedish woman lost her wedding ring while working in her kitchen. She looked for it everywhere, even pulling up the floor, and eventually gave up on finding it ever again. Sixteen years later she pulled a fresh carrot from her garden and found the missing ring, safely tucked around it. The only possible explanation is that the ring ended up among vegetable peelings that were worked into the garden at some time as compost.

Chefs' pleated headgear is designed to honor the French's love for eggs.

The 100 pleats in the high hat professional chefs wear (called a toque) are believed in culinary lore to refer to the 100 different ways French chefs could prepare eggs. The adage is generally attributed to the famous French chef of the 18th century, Auguste Escoffier.

The Scots have 421 words for snow.

According to academics at the University of Glasgow, the weather was extremely important to the livelihoods of the early Scottish people. Snow is a big part of the weather phenomena in this part of the world, and they needed to communicate very clearly about it. Some of their words include "feefle" (to swirl), "flindrikin" (a slight snow shower), and "snaw-pouther" (fine driving snow).

The longest English word has 189,819 letters.

Move over, "antidisestablishmentarianism." The full scientific name of the largest protein in the human body can't even be published in dictionaries because it would take up 12 pages. According to technical scientific guidelines, every amino acid contained in a protein has to be listed. The protein that is nicknamed "titin" contains 34,350 amino acids.

The expression "Murphy's Law" originated with a pessimistic sea captain.

The familiar expression of expecting the worst in a situation was more than a joke at the expense of pessimists; it was inspired by a real person. After testing a rocket sled at the Edwards Air Force Base in 1948, Captain Edward A. Murphy told his assistant to always expect someone to choose the disastrous option out of several possible ways to perform a task.

You could open a bar in space with the amount of alcohol present in cloud G34.3.

Astronomers found an interstellar gas cloud known as G34.3 that contains enough alcohol to produce 400 trillion trillion pints of beer, if it could be accessed. G34.3 is about 10,000 light-years away from earth, located in the huge constellation Aquila. If the alcohol could be harvested by humans, it would be enough to give every person on earth 300,000 pints of beer daily for the next billion years.

Humans are more similar to potatoes than you think.

In 2012, airplane manufacturer Boeing wanted to test the consistency of in-flight wireless signals in planes filled to capacity. They couldn't expect humans to sit motionless for days while they conduct their experiments, so they placed bags of fresh potatoes on the seats. The water content and chemistry of spuds let them absorb and reflect wi-fi signals just like human bodies do. The project was dubbed SPUDS: Synthetic Personnel Using Dialectic Substitution.

The smallest inhabited island on earth is aptly named "Just Enough Room."

At 3,300 square feet, the tiny piece of land is just off Alexandria Bay in New York state, on the St. Lawrence River. It was purchased in 1950 by the Sizelands family, who built a holiday cottage that fills the whole area, leaving only room for a tree and some deck chairs. To put the island's size in perspective, it is only slightly bigger than a tennis court.

Mushrooms are closer to animals and humans than to plants.

Genetic studies have shown that fungi and animals share a common ancestor, despite mushrooms having been classified as plants for many years. The two groups parted ways about 1.1 billion years ago, but they still share some proteins. DNA comparisons with plants show them to have followed an independent evolutionary track from fungi.

Sugar can help a wound heal faster.

Granules of sugar on a wound will soak up any moisture that creates a favorable environment for bacteria to thrive. Without bacteria, a wound can heal quicker. This can be especially helpful in the case of bacteria that resist antibiotics.

The right smell can help you lose weight.

A study done by the Smell and Taste Treatment and Research Foundation in Chicago, Illinois, found that overweight people who smelled green apples, bananas, grapefruit, vanilla, or peppermint when they were hungry had smaller appetites and lost weight faster. These smells are interpreted as neutral by our brains and that curbs appetite.

Floss your teeth to improve your memory.

According to research done in 2021, regular flossing can prevent the onset of dementia and slow down general cognitive decline in later years. The inflammation caused by tooth decay, as well as the poor diet of some older people who lost many of their teeth, are the main possible reasons for the correlation between oral and brain health.

There are more people speaking English as a second language than native English speakers.

It is estimated that about 1.5 billion people speak English, but less than 400 million use it as their first language. The Netherlands came out tops in terms of English proficiency in the 2019 English Proficiency Index, scoring 72 points.

Once a year, it rains fish in the small Honduran town of Yoro.

This is no tall fisherman's tale—several scientists have witnessed the event, but the exact cause is not yet known. Annually, after a heavy rainstorm, the townspeople find still-alive fish flopping around in their streets. Scientific theories about the strange phenomenon range from blaming waterspouts for picking up fish from the ocean, to proposing that fish living underground in the area are forced above ground by the storm.

The lowest temperature ever physically measured on earth was -129 °F (−89.2 °C).

On July 23, 1983, the ultra-low temperature was measured at Vostok Station in Antarctica. However, satellite data collected between 2004 and 2016 showed the region regularly plunged to about −138 °F (-94 °C).

The country with the most islands in the world is Sweden, with 267,570.

Most of these islands are along Sweden's east coast. About 24,000 of them are open to the public under the country's Right of Public Access policy. Fewer than 1,000 of the islands are inhabited.

Watching a horror movie can be literally bloodcurdling.

In the British Medical Journal's Christmas edition of 2015, a small study from the Netherlands appeared, showing that fear can significantly elevate a clotting protein in the blood called Factor VIII. Clotting proteins enable our blood to thicken and stop flowing in the event of an injury, and it seems our brains prepare our bodies for trauma when we get really scared.

The South Asian country Bangladesh has six official seasons.

Besides winter, summer, autumn, and spring, the country of Bangladesh—which lies to the east of India—also has a late autumn and a monsoon season. Late autumn is from mid-October to mid-December. The monsoon season, stretching from mid-June to mid-August, is mainly sub-tropically hot and humid.

It snows metal on the planet Venus.

Venus has impressive mountains with tops that seem to be covered in snow. The heat on the planet makes it impossible for snow, as we know it, to exist, though. The temperature on the plains goes up to 894°F (480°C). That vaporizes the pyrite minerals on the surface and they are deposited as a fine metallic mist on the tops of the mountains. When the mist condenses, a shiny frost-like "snow" is left behind.

Bedbugs lived alongside dinosaurs.

Those unwelcome little critters that sometimes share our beds are much older than scientists previously thought. They lived at the same time as the dinosaurs, about 100 million years ago. That means they evolved around 50 million years earlier than bats, who were believed to have been their first hosts.

The Canadian town of Fermont gets so cold that most of the structures in the town were designed to be interconnected.

The little mining town of Fermont, located in northeastern Quebec, Canada, experiences temperatures well below freezing during the seven-months-long winter. A wall-like structure containing interconnected houses, restaurants, stores, schools, bars, and a hotel was built on one side, ensuring that the residents won't need to go outdoors in the cold unless it is absolutely necessary.

You can laugh yourself to death.

For some people, laughing themselves to death can be more than just a figure of speech. The medical term for this rare occurrence is *laughter-induced syncope*. It happens when someone laughs so hard that the pressure inside the chest cavity increases drastically. That restricts the blood flow to the heart and the person experiences seizures before fainting and, after a few minutes, dying.

Tomatoes have more genes than humans.

With 35,000 genes, tomatoes definitely have the edge on humans, who have only 20,000 genes. But, before you start worrying about a "tomato takeover," researchers found that the number of genes were unrelated to the mental and emotional complexity of an organism.

A sneeze can send germs flying at 100 miles per hour.

Researchers have measured the droplets flying through the air after a person sneezed and found them to travel at about 100 miles per hour. In addition to their speed, their number of around 100,000 per sneeze can make it somewhat difficult to evade getting someone else's cold, if you're not quick.

Sardinian shepherds enjoy a creamy cheese that is produced by maggots as a delicacy.

The cheese, known as "casu marzu," is produced when cheese skipper flies lay their eggs in cracks in the salty Pecorino cheese that is also made in the area. After hatching, the maggots eat their way through the hard cheese and their digestion of the proteins transforms the insides of the cheese to a soft, creamy texture.

The heaviest onion ever grown so far weighed more than 18 lbs.

British gardener Peter Glazebrook broke the world record for the world's heaviest onion in 2012 at the Harrogate Flower Show in North Yorkshire. He entered a humongous vegetable weighing 18 lb 1 oz. That is more than 8 kg! Incidentally, Mr. Glazebrook also holds records for the longest beetroot, heaviest potato, and longest parsnip.

You can grow a whole fruit salad on one tree.

Thanks to the inventive thinking of Australians James and Kerry West, fruit salad trees were created in the early 1990s by multi-grafting different fruits from the same family onto one tree. The available fruit families include stone fruit, citrus, Asian pears, and apples.

The world's smallest functional guitar is only as big as a single human blood cell.

Cornell University researchers Harold G. Craighead and Dustin W. Carr fashioned the guitar in 1997 from crystalline silicon to demonstrate advances in nanotechnology. The guitar has six strings that resonate when force is exerted on them, but the frequency is inaudible to the human ear.

A study on the disappearance of teaspoons in the workplace was once published in Australia.

In 2005, students at the Macfarlane Burnet Institute for Medical Research and Public Health in Melbourne, Australia, became frustrated with the constant lack of teaspoons in their tearoom. They discreetly marked 16 new teaspoons, and after 5 months, 80% of the spoons had disappeared. The students published their findings, concluding (rather tongue-in-cheek) that developing effective control measures against teaspoon losses should be an important point on all national research agendas.

Hot peppers only burn because they trick our brains.

Chili peppers contain a chemical irritant called capsaicin. When the tissue or mucous membranes of any mammal come into contact with capsaicin, the sensory nerves of the mammal are tricked into believing they are on fire.

You can heat up a cup of coffee by yelling at it for 8 years, 7 months, 26 days, 20 hours, 26 minutes and 40 seconds.

When you yell, you release energy in the form of sound. The energy has to go somewhere because energy never gets destroyed. In a confined space, the sound energy will enter the coffee and eventually get converted to kinetic energy that will boil the liquid.

It is illegal to die on Norway's Svalbard archipelago.

The small land mass lies about halfway to the North Pole, off the coast of Norway. It is so cold there that nothing decomposes in the earth, not even the flu viruses from 1918 that scientists found alive in some of the bodies buried there. The town of Longyearbyen, situated on the archipelago, therefore made it illegal for anyone nearing the end of their lives to remain there.

Your stomach also blushes when your face does.

Blushing happens when blood rushes to the surface of the skin. The process is initiated by the sympathetic nervous system due to various triggers and it occurs throughout the body. The stomach lining contains a multitude of blood vessels, just like our faces, so it also turns bright red when our faces show a blush.

The human body glows.

In 2009, Japanese scientists using ultra-sensitive cameras recorded a bioluminescent glow around human bodies. The dim light is believed to be a side-effect of our metabolism; molecules of free radicals, lipids, and proteins interact with chemical compounds that can emit photons. Unfortunately, the intensity of the light is 1,000 lower than the lowest light our human eyes can detect.

China has an ancient underground forest, located in a deep sinkhole.

While you can be forgiven for thinking that the interior of a sinkhole will consist only of rocks and sand, a 630-feet-deep cavity discovered in China in May 2022 houses a giant forest. The space is about 1,000 feet in length and 490 feet wide. Some of the ancient trees are 131 feet tall, while several of the plant species lining the walls and floor of the sinkhole were previously unknown to science.

The biggest fungus on earth is as big as 1,665 football fields.

The *Armillaria ostoyae* was discovered in Oregon's Blue Mountains in 1998. At almost four square miles, it is bigger than the blue whale that had previously been thought to be the largest living organism on earth. Scientists estimate that the fungus could be as old as 8,650 years.

You could get killed by exploding seedpods if you had a sandbox tree in your garden.

The sandbox tree, also known as the dynamite tree, is a member of the spurge family and is native to South America. When the fruit of the tree dry out and become seed capsules, they explode upon maturity with a loud bang. The explosion sends the hard seeds hurling away at speeds of up to 150 mph, traveling more than 60 feet away from the tree.

Termites love rock music.

When rock music is played in the vicinity of wood structures, the wood starts vibrating at the same frequency as the music. Researchers in the mid 2000s found that termites munch twice as fast on wood with a hard rock vibration, which is in the range between 600 Hz and 3 kHz.

Israeli scientists taught a goldfish how to drive on land.

Shachar Givon, from Ben-Gurion University in Israel, and her colleagues put six goldfish in mobile aquariums that could be moved by the swimming motions of the fish. Once they mastered the movement, the fish were given treats when they navigated through obstacles to specific points. According to the researchers, it took the fish only a couple of days to master each new course.

The color you see when you open your eyes in the pitch dark has a name.

The darkish, uniformly gray background that most people see when they open their eyes in environments without any outside light is called *Eigengrau*. It is a German word from the 19th century meaning "intrinsic gray." The color results from signals generated by the optic nerves.

The population of the UK is outnumbered by chickens.

The estimated 66 million inhabitants of the UK eat about 982 million chickens each year. That means there are a whopping 14.87 chickens for every human.

Sponges can reconstruct themselves from fragments.

When the cells of these interesting marine creatures are separated by, for instance, pushing the animal through a fine mesh, the single cells migrate back toward each other and form clusters. The clusters attach themselves to flat surfaces where the cells rearrange themselves to form a young, new sponge, ready to grow.

The average annual rainfall of the city Arica in Chile is about as high as a flea egg.

The 1,000 miles wide Atacama desert on the coast of northern Chile is one of the most arid regions on earth. The Andes Mountains block virtually all the moist air systems that could have reached the area from the Amazon Basin. Atacama has several cities, some of which have not recorded a single drop of rain, ever. Arica, one of its largest cities, receives annual rainfall averaging only 0.03 inches (0.76 millimeters)— just about the height of a flea egg.

The oldest vegetables known are peas.

Remains of wild peas have been found in the region around the Mediterranean Sea that date to the late Neolithic Period, which occurred about 10,000 B.C.E. The domesticated version of the plant reached other parts of the world through European colonization.

A clover with 56 leaves on one stem was discovered in Japan.

A 4-leaf clover is supposed to bring good luck, but a Japanese man found a 56-leaf clover in 2009. Dr. Shigeo Obara of Hanamaki City has devoted his life to studying clover plants. He also found the previous record holder in 2002, a clover with 18 leaves.

The most poisonous plant in North America can kill a human with only a quarter-inch of its root.

Water hemlock (*Cicuta maculata*) that is native to the whole of North America is a perennial herb that can grow as tall as six feet.

Due to its root system of white tubers, it is sometimes mistaken for parsnips. Unfortunately, the highest concentration of its toxin is in the roots. Ingestion of even a small piece can cause the death of humans and livestock within half an hour.

A plant in the Philippines eats rats to supplement the poor soil quality.

Nepenthes rajah is the biggest example found so far of a species known as "pitcher plants." The giant plant, located in the central Philippines, has a long tendril that opens up to form a large cup filled with enzymes and acid. Nectar on the edges attracts insects and animals as large as rats. Once they've slid down the slippery sides, the plant closes a lid on the cup and digests its meal.

The smallest surviving premature baby weighed only 8.5 oz at birth.

Baby Saybie weighed as much as a large apple when she was born at 23 weeks and 3 days in California in December 2018. She was only nine inches in length. After spending five months in the hospital, she was discharged weighing a healthy 5.6 lbs.

Japan has the world's deepest underwater mailbox.

The unique mailbox is at a depth of almost 33 feet under the waters of Susami Bay. People buy waterproof cards and write their messages on them with oil-based paint markers, before diving down to place them in the red postbox. About 32,000 pieces of mail have been posted there to date.

Taylor Glacier in Antarctica oozes a rusty, red liquid.

The red water that seeps through a crack in the glacier is known as Blood Falls. It comes from a big lake under Taylor Glacier. The water is full of microbes and has a high iron content. As soon as the water comes into contact with air, it rusts, resulting in the red color.

Less than an ounce of the rarest naturally occurring material on Earth exists at any given moment.

Astatine is not only rare, but also unstable. Its longest-living isotope, astatine-210, has a half-life of just more than eight hours.

Baby planthopper insects have a functional gear system on their back legs to stabilize their bodies before they jump.

Planthopper nymphs in the *Issus* genus are the first animals known to use a fully functional gear system in their regular movements. The insect's back legs have protruding gear teeth on the inside edges. When the teeth of the gear mesh, the back legs are locked together and the body is stabilized. That helps the little guy to accelerate at an amazing 1/300,000 of a second.

Earth has an "evil" blue twin where it rains molten glass.

The blue planet HD189733-b looks just like the earth from a distance, but conditions there are much different. The wind blows at seven times the speed of sound, bringing with it a rain of molten glass. The planet is about 64.5 light-years away from our solar system, in the constellation of Vulpecula.

There is a type of fungus that eats radiation for breakfast (and lunch, and dinner!)

In 1991, scientists discovered an unknown type of fungus growing inside and around the Chernobyl nuclear power plant in Ukraine. It not only eats radioactive compounds, but thrives on radiation itself. Known simply as radiotrophic fungi, the organism uses a process similar to photosynthesis to convert gamma energy into usable chemical energy for its growth.

The biggest flower on earth is more than three feet wide.

The *Rafflesia Arnoldii*, also known as the Monster Flower, grows in the rainforests of Indonesia. It is a parasite that lives underground on the roots of other plants until it's ready to flower. The orange-yellow blooms grow to more than three feet across and can weigh up to fifteen pounds.

Coins are not smelly; we are.

The metallic smell on your hands after handling coins or other metal objects does not come from the metal. Its source is skin oil from our hands. The oils break down upon contact with iron, forming the organic molecule 1-octen-3-one and causing the characteristic smell.

The Cromwell chafer beetle has the smallest habitat on earth.

One of the rarest species on earth lives on just one small patch of land in Central Otago, in New Zealand. The flightless Cromwell chafer beetle is critically endangered, which is why the 200-acre area on the Cromwell river terrace, where the handful of specimens still alive are found, was declared a nature reserve in the early 1980s. It is the only nature reserve in the world proclaimed for an invertebrate.

African dung beetles are the only insects known to use the Milky Way to navigate at night.

International scientists studying the African dung beetle observed them walking in a straight line to their nests to deposit the dung they collected, even on moonless nights. In an experiment, the scientists tied tiny visors to the beetles' faces that blocked their view of the starry night sky. The insects wandered around aimlessly until the visors were removed and they could see the Milky Way again.

The morpho dragonfly's wings are alive.

The wings on all young insects are fully alive. The cells in the wings gradually die as the insects grow into adulthood, until only the veins running through them are supported by life systems. When looking at the wings of a male morpho dragonfly under a microscope, however, scientists saw respiratory tubes. The only possible conclusion they could arrive at is that morpho dragonflies have wings that remain alive.

Radiation can change a person's eye color.

Several cancer patients have experienced a change in the hue of their eyes after strong radiation therapy. Another well-known example of this effect of radiation was noted after the Chernobyl nuclear disaster in Ukraine. Vladimir Pravik was one of the first firefighters on the scene. During his subsequent hospitalization for 16 days before he died of radiation exposure, it was noted that his eyes changed from brown to blue.

The island country of Papua New Guinea represents 12% of all the languages spoken worldwide.

Although considered a small country, at 178,700 square miles, about 840 different languages are spoken by the almost 9 million inhabitants of this island in the southwestern Pacific Ocean. A possible reason for the great linguistic diversity is the isolation of the region. A number of the languages are endangered, however, with less than 100 speakers.

Tattoos don't live in the skin; they live in the immune system.

Tattoos are notoriously difficult to remove. That is because their ink goes much deeper than just skin cells. When the tattoo is applied, white blood cells rush to the site to repair the injury and absorb the foreign substance—the ink, in this case. The blood cells can't break down the ink, so they stay in place to protect the skin. When they die, other cells appear to consume the released ink, keeping the tattoo in place.

Hiccups may be historic leftovers from the gills we don't have anymore.

Getting the hiccups can be very irritating; it's even more annoying when you realize no one really knows what causes them. A couple of theories about why they happen have emerged over the years. One of these is that hiccupping is a mechanism we needed in our amphibian days, when we still had gills, as well as lungs. A well-timed hiccup was needed to close the glottis, allowing water to bypass the lungs and go to the gills.

CHaPTeR 5: TeCHnOLOGY

You can still visit the very first website ever made.

Tim Berners-Lee, a British scientist, created the World Wide Web and built the first website in 1989. He created this on his NeXT Computer while working for CERN, the European Organization for Nuclear Research. It was meant as a way for scientists and universities to share information with each other. If you visit the site today, it will look archaic, but it describes the project in detail. Without that site, the internet would have been a much different place than we know today. The site can be accessed on info.cern.ch/hypertext/WWW/TheProject.html.

Americans throw away $60 million in gold and silver every year.

Every year, new mobile phones are released, and most people jump at the chance to get hold of the latest model. That usually means the old phone finds its new home in a drawer or, most likely, the dumpster. In America, 14 million mobile devices are thrown away every year. Unfortunately, very few people realize exactly what they are throwing away. Besides toxic waste, phones contain precious metals like gold and silver. Would you throw $60 million in the garbage if you knew?

E-mail existed long before the World Wide Web.

In the 1960s, Ray Tomlinson invented electronic mail. It was more of an in-house project as opposed to the email we know today, but the idea was there. Another fun fact is that the first spam email was sent in 1978 by Gary Rhuerk to several hundred users on the ARPANET (Advanced Research Projects Agency Network).

A famous actress invented Wi-Fi.

Where would modern technology have been without Wi-Fi? Hedy Lamarr was a stunning actress, but her love of tinkering and WWII would see her take a break from acting to focus her energy on helping the war efforts. She had heard about the problems the Navy was having with radio-controlled torpedoes; so she, along with composer George Antheil, created the Secret Communication System. The idea behind the invention was to have a system that constantly changed frequencies, making it difficult to decode. Unfortunately, the Navy did not accept this patent because it was ahead of its time, and they thought it was too complex. They also rejected it because it had been made by a civilian—not just any civilian, but an actress. It wasn't until the 1960s that the Navy finally started using the technology. It went on to pave the way for the Bluetooth and, ultimately, the Wi-Fi technology we know today.

The Navy uses video game controllers.

The periscopes on modern submarines are remotely controlled, but the official control unit costs upward of $40,000. Not to mention, the control is not user-friendly, and it can take sailors hours to master operating it. The Navy decided to switch to Xbox 360 controllers, instead. Microsoft must have done something right; the sailors say the game controllers are lighter, more intuitive, and way easier to use. The average cost for such a console is around $20 now, which makes it much cheaper to replace when a new one is needed. Training time was also reduced from hours to mere minutes.

There is a butt-shaped robot that is used to test phones.

No, this robot is not testing ways to prevent those awkward phone calls. Most of us have experienced the pain of ending up with a broken mobile, or a cracked screen, after sitting down on a phone that stayed forgotten in a back pocket. Samsung came up with a "butt robot" to test the durability of their phones. The robot sits down on the phone, repeatedly, to see how long the product can withstand the abuse.

There is only one computer that is acceptable to the Amish.

For most of us, the Amish are people who refuse to take part in the modern world and its ways. Generally speaking, they have no use for the gadgets and technologies we love, such as the internet. However, there is one computer that is specifically marketed for them. The machine is used for business, and business only. The Amish rules aren't as strict as they once were. That makes the Amish people more willing to adopt something modern if they can justify the need for it, and as long as they can keep it out of their homes.

The first vacuum cleaner was so big it had to be drawn by a horse.

"Puffing Billy," the nickname given to the first petrol-driven cleaner that used suction power to remove dust, was designed by Hubert Cecil Booth in 1901. The noisy machine was very bulky and had to be drawn by a horse. It became very popular, however, and was even used to clean the carpets at Westminster Abbey in preparation for the coronation of Edward VII in August 1902.

The shortest commercial flight lasts only 90 seconds.

Yes, you read that right. A flight between Scotland's islands Westray and Papa Westray is only 1.7 miles long and takes a mere 90 seconds to complete. Although short, the flight—that has been around since 1967—is a lifeline for locals in the remote areas. Teachers, school kids, health staff, and residents all need Loganair's unique flight to get to and from the mainland.

Google was initially called "BackRub."

Larry Page and Sergey Brin created what has become today's most popular search engine in 1996, calling it "BackRub." That was a reference to the way the system analyzes backlinks to determine a site's rankings. A year later, the search engine processed so much data that the creators needed to upgrade the name. The name "Google" was derived from the number "googolplex," which is the digit "1" followed by a "googol" (10,100) zeroes.

Singapore has a car vending machine.

The 15-story building belongs to Gary Hong, who spent many boyhood hours daydreaming with his Matchbox cars. The structure contains 60 high-end luxury cars, such as Bentleys and Ferraris, in brightly lit compartments. Customers choose their car from a touch display in the street, and the vehicle is brought down to them in minutes through a complex series of gears and platforms.

A Japanese vegetable juice maker invented a wearable robot that feeds tomatoes to marathon runners.

Juice company Kagome believes tomatoes are the best sustenance you can get when running a marathon. Enter *Tomatan*: a wearable, tomato-headed, robot backpack. At the flip of a switch, the robot will grab a tomato from its stash, swing its metal arms over your head, and feed the juicy treat to you.

Bluetooth was named after a Viking king.

King Harald "Bluetooth" Gormsson lived in the 10th century. He loved eating blueberries, and his nickname came from his blue-stained teeth. He united Denmark and Norway. The creators of the Bluetooth technology view it as a "uniter" of devices, hence the Bluetooth name.

Electronics giant Samsung started as a company selling vegetables, dry fish, and noodles.

Korean businessman Byung-Chull Lee started his company in 1938 as an exporter of Korean goods to China. They branched out to textiles and insurance in the early 1950s. Their first black-and-white TV was only released on the market in 1970. This sold so well that they turned to electronic goods and household appliances, exclusively.

Sir David Attenborough holds the record for the longest TV presenter.

With a career spanning 70 years, British naturalist and broadcaster Sir David Attenborough started as a presenter with the BBC in 1952. He is the only one who received BAFTA awards for black-and-white series, color filma, HD, and 3D formats.

The QWERTY keyboard was developed to make the lives of Morse code technicians easier.

Japanese researchers concluded in 2011 that the well-known design of the QWERTY keyboard was not meant to slow the typist down, as many people believe, but rather to speed things up. Telegraphic operators working in Morse code found it confusing when the letter keys were in alphabetical order. The QWERTY keyboard layout that was adopted in the 1910s helped Morse code receivers and senders to keep up with each other's speeds.

Only about eight percent of all the currency used globally is physical money.

Economists agree that at least 92% of the money used in global transactions today exists only digitally. Most transactions are conducted with cards or apps. This means that money mostly lives only on computer hard drives and servers.

One of the earliest Russian computers ran on water.

Russian engineer Vladimir Sergeevich Lukyanov built a computer in 1936 that was known as the Water Integrator. It used a complex series of interconnected tubes and pumps, housed in a cabinet as big as a closet. The water levels in the tubes represented various stored values, and the speed at which the levels interacted with each other represented mathematical processes. The results were plotted in a graph.

Google hires goats as gardeners.

Instead of getting noisy and smelly lawn mowers to mow their lawn, the guys at Google's Mountain View, California, headquarters hire 200 goats, once a month, to keep their lawn trimmed. A herder from the company California Grazing brings them to the building, and a border collie named Jen guards them.

The first videocassette recorder (VCR) was the size of a piano.

Built in 1956 by the Ampex Company, it was the brainchild of Charles Ginsburg, who became known as the father of the videocassette recorder. It used two-inch tape and cost $50,000. Due to the high cost, it could initially only be afforded by television networks and the largest individual stations.

The first computer mouse was a rectangular wooden box with two metal wheels.

Douglas Engelbart invented the first mouse in 1964. The two wheels could move in only one direction, and the device had one button on the wooden housing. When asked why it was called a mouse, Engelbart replied that the wire coming out of the box just reminded him of a rodent's tail.

You had to get up at four in the morning if you wanted an alarm clock in 1787.

The first alarm clock was made in 1787 by Levi Hutchins. There was just one drawback: it could only ring at four o'clock in the morning. The first wind-up version of an alarm clock that could be set for any time wasn't invented until 1876.

Yahoo!'s original URL was akebono.standford.edu

The search engine Yahoo! was launched in 1994 by two men who were electrical engineering students at Stanford University at the time, Jerry Yang and David Filo. It was originally called "Jerry and David's Guide to the World Wide Web." The pair renamed it to Yahoo! when it rose in popularity.

The word "android" refers only to males.

Although used interchangeably for both male and female, an android actually refers to a robot with a male human appearance. The female equivalent of an android is called a "gynoid."

Senior internet users are called Silver Surfers.

Many older people tend to stay away from computers, the internet, and technology in general. There are, however, always exceptions to any rule. People over 50 years of age who regularly use the internet have become known as Silver Surfers.

Carrier pigeons once beat the internet for speed.

In September 2010, residents in a rural area of the UK staged a stunt to demonstrate to the government that broadband access outside of cities was not good enough. They attached a USB stick with 50 GB of data to a carrier pigeon, and let it go at the same time they started an upload of the same amount of data. The pigeon won the race by almost an hour.

CHapter 6: Famous and Infamous People

The mastermind behind the notorious Bonnie and Clyde criminal pair was Clyde's mother.

Contrary to popular belief, Clyde Barrow's mother was more than a protective, loving relative. The prosecutor in the trial that followed the pair's death, Clyde O. Eastus, alleged during his closing argument that Cumie Barrow was the mastermind behind the couple's bloody two-year criminal spree. Nobody believed him at the time, but new scrutiny of history showed her to have been a manipulative, lying woman who often made payoffs to keep her son and Bonnie Parker out of prison, as well as spinning stories to reporters to throw the police off their trail.

The French military and political leader Napoleon Bonaparte once lost a battle to a horde of bunnies.

The famous conqueror suffered one defeat that was even more embarrassing than Waterloo. It happened in 1807, when the emperor asked his chief of staff to arrange a rabbit hunt for himself and his men. Instead of snaring wild hares, the men rounded up about 3,000 tame bunnies. When they were released from their cages, the bunnies charged straight at Napoleon and his men, expecting the humans to feed them. Napoleon had to beat a hasty retreat, with bunnies clinging to his legs and some even making it into his coach.

The "Mad Monk" of Russia, Rasputin, survived being poisoned, shot, and beaten during his assassination.

During the early 1900s, the mystic Grigori Rasputin befriended the last emperor of Russia, Nicholas II, and his family. Rasputin gained great influence in matters of state, making the Russian nobles very uncomfortable. They hatched a plan to kill Rasputin and lured him to the Yusupov Palace, giving him food and wine laced with cyanide. When the poison failed to kill him, they shot him at close range and left him for dead. Still alive, Rasputin attempted to leave the palace. He was shot and beaten again, but when the nobles examined his body, he had still not died. Exasperated, they tossed him into the freezing cold nearby river where, finally, he perished. His cause of death was most likely hypothermia.

One of the most ruthless leaders of the 20th century, Joseph Stalin, had his enemies removed from photographs.

When the former Soviet leader Joseph Stalin took over power in 1929, he started what became known as the "Great Purge" campaign. He used the campaign to rid himself of anyone who opposed his leadership. Thousands of people died and many were exiled during this purge. To consolidate his power, Stalin also made sure that no records of his enemies remained in existence. The dictator hired photo retouchers to erase all of them from photographs, including many of his own party's officials and trusted people. Any images that survived until today, depicting Stalin on his own before he became the Soviet leader, were most likely edited years ago.

The belongings of the French physicist famous for her work on radioactivity, Marie Curie, are still "radiating" her life's work.

Marie Curie's work with atomic particles claimed for her an illustrious career, two Nobel Prizes, and the inspiration of women from all over the world to pursue their passion in science. She and her husband discovered radium and polonium, but the long-term exposure to these elements eventually brought about Curie's death. All her belongings are kept inside lead-lined containers because of the huge amounts of radiation they were exposed to. Unfortunately, the half-life of radium 266 is around 1,600 years. That means visitors to the exhibit of her life and work have to wear protective suits and sign a waiver at the Bibliotheque Nationale in Paris before they're allowed to view any of the items.

Pirates' eye patches had nothing to do with losing an eye.

While it is historically correct that pirates wore eye patches, the reason for doing so is not related to battle scars, at all. Pirates often had to adjust quickly between the daylight on the ship's deck and the darkness below deck. Closing one eye with a patch ensured they always had at least one eye that was instantly ready for action in the dark.

Pirate earrings were not for fashion purposes, either.

No depiction of a pirate would be accurate without a golden earring dangling from at least one ear. Contrary to popular belief, they didn't wear the jewelry to be fashionable. They believed pressure on the ear lobe could cure any seasickness.

The famous Austrian composer of classical music, Wolfgang Amadeus Mozart, was a shopaholic.

The beloved composer of timeless music had a vice that we know all too well today. He loved shopping and spent huge amounts on lavish clothing to keep up his flamboyant style. Despite earning around 10,000 florins a year, which is around $42,000 today, he died poor and received only a pauper's burial.

Stephen King almost scrapped his entire first novel.

Who knows where the famous horror writer would be if he hadn't written "Carrie?" He almost found out, though. After writing only three pages of the novel, he threw everything in the trash. He didn't think he could write about the life of a teenage girl. His wife, however, dug the pages out and encouraged him to keep at it, promising to provide a female perspective if he needed it. King turned those three pages into the novel we know today. After the book's first edition, the paperback rights sold for almost half a million dollars. "Carrie" became the start of King's hugely successful writing career.

Japanese engineer Tsutomu Yamaguchi survived both atomic bombings during WWII.

In 1945, Yamaguchi spent three months in Hiroshima on a business trip as an engineer for Mitsubishi. On his last day there, the first atomic bomb fell with Yamaguchi a mere two miles from the center of the explosion. He regained consciousness after a while and returned to Nagasaki the next day. While trying to convince his superior at the Mitsubishi office that a bomb really devastated Hiroshima, the second bomb exploded with Yamaguchi surviving once more being less than two miles from ground zero.

Peter the Great, the ruler of Russia from 1682 until 1725, imposed a tax on his subjects for permission to have facial hair.

Peter I, better known as Peter the Great, toured Europe in 1697-1698 in disguise to try and learn from the imperial successes in countries such as England and the Netherlands. Upon his return, he started modernizing Russia. He changed the way the Russian language was written, revised the calendar, and tried to convince ordinary Russians to go clean-shaven like the Europeans. To encourage the adoption of his beard reforms, the ruler introduced a beard tax in exchange for the right to wear a beard.

Actor and politician Arnold Schwarzenegger once had a very successful bricklaying business.

The well-known bodybuilder, actor, and eventually governor of California started his rags-to-riches story with a business venture. Schwarzenegger and Franco Columbo opened their bricklaying business in 1968, when Arnold was just 21 years old. The demand for materials rose after the San Fernando earthquake in 1971, and the two partners' business became hugely successful. Columbo later turned out to become the man who took the Mr. Olympia crown from Schwarzenegger in 1976.

Rockstar David Bowie released his own internet service provider, "BowieNet."

David Bowie often declared that he thought the internet would become one of the wonders of the world. He understood the potential of the system, both the good and the bad. On two separate occasions, he contributed to its development. One of those was the creation of his own internet service provider (ISP) called "BowieNet." Released in 1998, users were given 20 MB to build their own homepage for a small monthly fee. The ISP lasted until 2012. The other was when Bowie became the first major artist to release a song that could be downloaded. "Telling Lies" was released exclusively on his website, and it was downloaded more than 300,000 times.

The Guinness Book of World Records holds a record of its own.

This book, which has kept us spellbound with marvelous world records since 1955, is the book stolen most often from public libraries worldwide. Despite the copies lost to readers with long fingers, though, more than 143 million copies in over 100 countries have already been sold. The book has also been translated into more than 22 languages.

Autographs served as insurance for the Apollo 11 astronauts.

Going into space is a risky business, and no insurance company was prepared to sell life insurance to Neil Armstrong and the rest of the Apollo 11 crew before their historic trip to the moon in 1969. To provide for their families, in case they didn't make it back from the moon alive, the three astronauts signed hundreds of autographs that their families could sell if the worst happened to them.

The world record for the most T-shirts worn at the same time is 260.

Canadian Ted Hastings secured his place in the Guinness Book of World Records in February 2019 by putting on 260 T-shirts over each other. The shirts ranged in size from medium to 20X.

About 16 million of the men alive today are direct descendants of the infamous ruler of the Mongol Empire, Genghis Khan.

Genghis Khan was, among other things, infamous for waging countless brutal wars and fathering children with as many of the females from the conquered lands as possible. The warlord lived between 1162 and 1227. A 2003 study found that 0.5% of all males alive in the world today carry Genghis's Y-chromosome. That boils down to about one in every 200 men.

Ashrita Furman from New York holds the record for setting the most records.

Since 1997, Ashrita Furman has set more than 700 world records. He currently holds more than 200 of them, also breaking the record for the individual holding the most records at the same time.

The famous artist Salvador Dali avoided paying restaurant tabs by doodling on the checks.

When taking out friends or students for a large meal at a restaurant, Dali usually offered to pay for everything. After writing the check, he quickly drew something on the back of the check with the waiter watching. He knew the owner would never cash such a valuable drawing!

Albert Einstein hated socks.

The famous mathematician refused to wear socks, even to a meeting with President Franklin Delano Roosevelt at the White House. Einstein told reporters that, as a child, his big toe often poked a hole in his socks. His protruding toe irritated him to the point where he decided to do away with the foot garments altogether as soon as he entered adulthood.

CHAPTER 7: ANIMALS AND INSECTS

A cow is deadlier than a shark.

As deadly and feared as they are, sharks only kill about four people worldwide per year. In comparison, the creature that kills an average of 22 people annually is the cow. The cause of death is mostly goring or stomping.

The pistol shrimp makes a noise louder than a gunshot.

Believe it or not, one of the loudest animals alive is a crustacean that only grows to approximately 2 centimeters (0.787 inch) long. The pistol shrimp has a huge snapper that can be shut so fast (at about 60 mph) that it creates a stream of bubbles shooting out at 25 miles per second. The bubbles stun the prey, and when they disintegrate, a sonic boom like a gunshot can be heard. The shock wave has been measured at 210 decibels. In comparison, a real gunshot only measures between 165 and 175 decibels. The only ocean creatures louder than pistol shrimps are sperm whales that click at around 230 decibels.

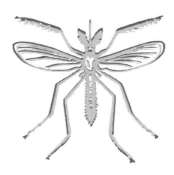

Mosquitoes are the deadliest creatures on earth.

Cows might be deadlier than sharks, but if we take a worldwide view, mosquitoes are far more deadly than cows, sharks, bears, and tigers. Unlike other deadly animals you may think of, the little bloodsuckers are responsible for at least 725,000 deaths every year. With more than 2,500 species, they are found in every part of the globe. Their weapon of choice is the transfer of diseases like malaria, the West Nile Virus, and yellow fever.

The kangaroo rat never needs to drink water.

First things first, while they are named after the Australian animal, kangaroo rats have never been to the land down under. They are natives of the Nevada desert and got their names from their powerful hind legs that allow them to jump up to nine feet at a time. Although the desert is a very hot and dry place to live at the best of times, kangaroo rats don't need to drink water, ever. They obtain all the hydration they need to survive from the seeds they eat. On top of that, their kidneys are so efficient that their urine is extremely concentrated. They are able to get rid of waste materials without the need for lots of water to flush the kidneys.

If roosters could hear themselves, they would be deafened by their own crows.

With a rooster's crow hitting around 100 decibels, chances are they would all have gone deaf without their built-in ear protection. When they tilt their heads back and open their beaks fully to crow, a quarter of their ear canals close completely. Soft tissue also covers half of their eardrums. That avoids them being deafened by their own crows.

One 14-block section of New York City boasts its own ant.

No kidding! The "ManhattAnt" only exists in one section of the Big Apple and nowhere else on our planet. It is similar to a simple cornfield ant, but when studied, scientists found it matched no other ant species in the world. The researchers believe the ant evolved while being isolated from other insects within the massive city.

An eagle bankrupted a scientific study by racking up an exorbitant text-messaging bill.

The Russian Raptor Research and Conservation Network had a great idea. They were going to attach a text-based tracking device to 13 Steppe eagles to study their behavior. One of the eagles flew as far as Iran, which incurred a hefty roaming fee on the tracking device for the text messages that came through. To get an idea of how much this one bird cost the study, the roaming charge per text message would have been around $0.77. The eagle sent hundreds of messages at once, which ultimately caused the study to go bankrupt.

One breed of crow doesn't only use tools, but makes them as well.

Using tools requires the right cognitive skills, and in the early 1960s, Jane Goodall proved wild chimpanzees had the skills required. However, these primates are not the only animals that can do this. A non-primate species proved that not only could they use tools, but they could make them, as well. The honor goes to the New Caledonian crows. This species of corvid uses sticks or other things to dig insects from small spaces. If they can't find a ready-made digging tool, they make their own by trimming the leaves from sticks to create hook-shaped tools.

Wood frogs can freeze themselves.

Wood frogs inhabit a large part of North America, with the majority of them living in the forests of Canada and Alaska. The icy winter months experienced in these regions can be particularly dangerous for a frog. However, the wood frog's answer to the harsh conditions is a type of protein in its blood that causes the water in its body to freeze. During the freezing process, the frog's liver produces large amounts of glucose that protect its cells. This allows the frog's body to dehydrate, while all brain and heart activity cease. Once the weather warms up again, the frogs thaw, activating their internal organs. Before long, they are hopping along happily again through the woods.

African elephants have a sound specifically warning about human presence.

Researchers in Kenya found a group of resting elephants and began playing a recording of local people talking. The elephants made a sound like a low rumble. The sound was repeated a few times until the elephants got restless and moved away. The researchers then played a recording of that rumble to a different group of elephants and they promptly left the area.

Koalas have unique fingerprints like humans.

It's not just their adorableness and sweet demeanor that make us love these marsupials. We actually share the trait of unique fingerprints with them. When viewed under a microscope, the koala's fingerprints have the same loops and whirls that ours do. It is not so easy to distinguish a koala fingerprint from a human one. Australian crime investigators regard a crime scene contaminated if a koala tampered with it. Researchers believe they developed in this way to climb the eucalyptus trees where they forage for food more effectively.

Bees go silent during a solar eclipse.

Candace Galen, an ecologist at the University of Missouri, was curious about the possible influence a solar eclipse could have on bees. On the eve of the 2018 eclipse in the area, she placed microphones in 16 flower patches to record the bees. Upon analyzing the data, she found that the bees continued buzzing during the partial stages of the eclipse. The buzzes lasted longer, which suggested that the bees were taking longer flights and flying slower. When the total eclipse set in, the bees fell abruptly silent. As soon as the moon moved away and the sun came out again, the buzzing resumed.

The planthopper bug has gears in its legs.

The first gear made by a human was produced by a Greek mechanic around 300 B.C.E., but nature had already been using a gear system in insects. The *issus coleoptratus* is known as the planthopper bug and it was the first creature discovered with a gear system in its body. When the bugs are getting ready to jump, they position their legs in a ready-to-jump position. Tiny gears at the top of their legs then interlock and their legs rotate simultaneously. The planthopper bug's leap pulls an astonishing G-factor of 400 to reach a top speed of eight miles per hour.

One of Australia's caterpillars uses its old heads as a hat.

The *Uraba lugens* moth has a very creative defense in its caterpillar stage when it is known as the "gum-leaf skeletonizer" or, if you like puns, the "Mad Hatterpillar." It develops like all other caterpillars by shedding its outer shell. However, each time it sheds, it keeps the part of the shell where its head once was. Each molt adds a *hat* to this stack until it towers up in the air. They use the stack to bat away insects wanting to make a meal out of them.

The Oriental hornet can turn solar energy into electricity.

The Oriental hornet is just like all other hornets. It's mean, it'll attack you without provocation, and it looks terrifying. But, these insects come with one special feature. They can turn solar energy into electricity within their exoskeletons. The sun's rays enter their bodies through stripes on their abdomens. The yellow pigment in the stripes transforms the solar energy into electricity. They use the power for movement, as well as temperature regulation.

One snake steals poison from toxic toads.

One species of Asian snake is non-poisonous, but becomes poisonous because of its diet of toxic toads. The snake stores the toxins in its neck glands for later defensive use of its own. Biologists regard this as extremely rare conduct for a snake; this type of defense is usually only found in animals lower on the food chain, like insects and frogs. The snakes can also pass the toxin to their babies. It will last long enough to protect the young ones until they can hunt by themselves.

The brain of a cat is almost identical to ours.

While not a perfect match, the similarities are about 90%. A common misconception is that a bigger brain equates to higher intelligence, but size has got nothing to do with it. It has more to do with how the brain is folded and structured. That means cats are incredibly smart. Their independent way of thinking sometimes irks us, but don't be fooled. Cats evaluate everything and they simply refuse to engage in any activities that aren't rewarding to them.

You can't beat a catfish for taste.

Catfish, with their feline-like whiskers, have more than 100,000 taste buds all over their bodies, with the biggest concentration on the whiskers. That allows them to taste when food is near and zoom in on it accurately.

One Alaskan town had a feline honorary mayor for 20 years.

A town named Talkeetna had no human mayor, but from 1997 to 2017, a ginger cat named Stubbs served as honorary mayor to the town's 772 residents. He became a well-known and beloved symbol of the town with fans from around the globe.

Dolphins give each other names.

Researchers have identified unique whistles in dolphin pods that act like signatures. Specific whistles, every time, get the attention of the same animals. When a signature whistle is played to a dolphin, it responds by coming closer, as if to say, "Did you call my name?"

March 3rd is international "Be thankful your pets don't have opposable thumbs" Day.

Pet owner Thomas Roy and his wife, Ruth, came up with this celebration in the 1990s to remind us how grateful we should be that our pets can't open cans or doors themselves. Opposable Thumbs Day is only one of more than 90 holidays the Roys created.

There are two known species of water animal that never grow old.

The jellyfish *Turritopsis dohrnii* is scientifically known as biologically immortal because of its ability to revert to a previous stage of life at will, in response to stressful circumstances. The *Hydra*, a freshwater animal with an adhesive "foot" at one end and a mouth with tentacles at the other end, have a unique set of genes called FoxO. These genes enable hydras to constantly regenerate all their cells without aging.

Mosquitoes don't like noisy, modern music.

Recent research revealed that food-deprived yellow fever mosquitoes who were exposed to 10 minutes of excessively loud, modern music with a constantly escalating pitch did not feed on the blood of a captive hamster, or mate, while the noise was going on. Maybe modern music can be used as a natural alternative to pesticides, to prevent the spread of deadly diseases transferred through the bites of mosquitoes.

A woodpecker's tongue acts like a seatbelt for its brain during hard pecking.

Woodpeckers have amazingly long tongues for their body size. So long, in fact, that it has to be stored wrapped around the bird's brain. When the bird contracts the muscles supporting the tongue to stick it out, the combination of the tongue and muscles keeps the skull and spine firmly in place. That prevents injury during the high-speed pecking, much like a seat belt protects us in a vehicle.

Basenji dogs can't bark.

The Basenji is a breed of hunting dog that originated in Africa. They are also known as the "barkless dogs" because of their inability to make a real barking sound, although they are far from quiet. The internal structure of their throats is different to other dogs, and their vocal folds cannot vibrate enough to produce a classic bark. Instead, they howl, shriek, and meow with sounds that have been described as yodel-like.

India has Technicolor squirrels.

The Malabar giant squirrel is endemic to India. Its striking coat is brightly colored with maroon, brown, orange, and black. They grow to about three feet in length, which is much larger than other squirrels.

The smallest monkey on earth is only about as long as a toothbrush.

The pygmy marmoset has an average length of just over five inches. Adults weigh about three-and-a-half ounces. They live in the Amazon basin in family groups of one male, one female, children, and (possibly) one other adult.

The world's smallest bat is the size of a bumblebee.

Kitti's hog-nosed bat, also known as the bumblebee bat, is native to Thailand and Myanmar. They are a completely unique species called the Craseonycteridae. The miniscule animals were only discovered in 1974.

Honeybee queens not only buzz, but also quack and toot.

Besides the familiar buzzing sound, scientists observed new honeybee queens about to hatch making a distinct quacking sound. Once she's chewed her way out of the waxy cocoon she was in, she starts tooting until she leaves the nest, with about half the workers, to start her own nest. Researchers believe the tooting is a signal to the worker bees to delay the hatching of any other new queens until this one has left, to avoid them fighting to the death for domination.

conclusion

We might have reached the end of the book, but this is just the starting point in the genre I love so much. I still have many more facts for you from the books I've read, the travels I've experienced, and 26 years of following pop culture.

There are several more books to come, and I couldn't be more excited for you to get your hands on them.

Of course, this wouldn't be my kind of trivia book if I just left you with a basic, "Thanks for reading. Leave a review, and come back for the next book!" No! You are here for mind blowing facts, so here are a few more of them as a bonus to round off the adventure.

One couple wanted to name their baby "Brfxxccxxmnpcccll-Immnprxvclmnckssqlbb111116".

We've all shook our heads at the crazy names some celebrities give their children. This fashion, however, sometimes crops up among regular people, too. A Swedish couple wanted to call their child "Brfxxccxxmnpcccll-Immnprxvclmnckssqlbb111116" when he was born in 1996, saying the pronunciation would be "Albin." Sweden's laws regarding names are strict, and the name was rejected. In 2008, the parents were fined $682 for failing to register a legal name for their child before his fifth birthday.

A parking space in Hong Kong sold for almost $1 million.

If you live in a large city, you know the headache of paying for parking just to get to your office. In Hong Kong, it is almost impossible to find a good spot to park close to the city's fifth-tallest building, The Center. Businessman Johnny Cheung managed to get ownership of some parking spaces and started selling them off. Three of them sold in the six-figure range. For the fourth spot, an unknown buyer paid $969,000 just to be a little closer to work.

Cavities used to be a sign of wealth.

In the 18th century, sugar was a valuable commodity. Those who could get hold of it consumed it often and, in some cases, excessively. Too much sugar inevitably caused tooth cavities. The bacteria that caused the cavities made the affected teeth look black. Anyone from that era with a black tooth was regarded as wealthy, since sugar was so expensive.

Genghis Khan established one of the first international postal systems.

One of the major reasons for the success Genghis Khan's armies had was their excellent communication capabilities. Early on, Genghis established a courier service called the Yam. The Yam gradually grew into a full military postal service. It crossed multiple borders with a complete network of halfway stations and a central office, much like the modern post office.

A horned toad was entombed for more than three decades and lived.

This may seem like a tall tale from the state of Texas, but Old Rip—the horned toad—found himself in the wrong place at the wrong time. In 1897, the town of Eastland was building their courthouse when the little animal scurried across. No one took notice of him, and they ended up sealing him into one of the cornerstones of the building. Old Rip stayed there for 31 years until the courthouse was demolished. When the cornerstone was opened, the intrepid lizard was found, still very much alive. This made him so famous that the city had him embalmed and displayed in a tiny open casket in their new courthouse, when he finally died.

After 1944, all British tanks were equipped to make tea.

Tea is highly popular in England and has always been. Prior to 1944, the crews of military tanks had to exit the armored vehicle when they wanted to make a cup of tea. That made it possible, for example, for a couple of German Tiger tanks to destroy 30 British tanks in 15 minutes during WWII. The tanks had all been parked and left unattended for the British soldiers' tea break. This was highly embarrassing, and the crews realized they had to avoid becoming sitting ducks again. The next model of British tank—the Centurion, that was released in 1945—was equipped with a boiler inside the tank that was powered by the tank's electric circuits.

Rocket countdowns were inspired by a sci-fi movie.

If you have ever watched a rocket taking off, you are familiar with the countdown. Did you know that the idea for the countdown was taken from a silent sci-fi movie? In the 1929 film, *Frau im Mond*, Fritz Lang used a countdown to create suspense for the film's rocket launch scene. NASA used the movie as inspiration, years later. The only difference is that NASA can pause the countdown clock at any time if there are any mechanical difficulties or emergencies.

The French protected their capital city during WWI with a fake one.

Given our sophisticated radar and the highly detailed maps available today, we'll probably never get the chance to see this type of marvel again. During the two World Wars, however, things were different. Cities switched off all their lights at night to avoid making themselves a target for bombers. That made large areas in many countries pitch-black at night. France wanted to confuse German planes in their air space, so to protect Paris, they built a fake city. It was complete with a replica of the Champs-Elysées and Gare Du Nord. They even built a fake railway that lit up in certain areas to simulate a train moving along the tracks.

American park ranger Roy Sullivan survived being struck by lightning on seven different occasions.

While on duty in 1942, Roy Sullivan's lookout tower got struck several times by lightning. When he made a run for safety, he was struck in the leg. He survived, losing only a toenail. Lightning found him again in 1969, 1970, 1972, 1973, and 1976. By this time, Sullivan was ready for retirement, and he and his wife moved to Virginia. While out fishing, he got hit for the seventh time. Despite sustaining some injuries this time, Sullivan survived, yet again.

Now, we have *really* reached the end. I hope these facts will have you ready to tackle *Jeopardy*, or at least be enough for new talking points at your future gatherings.

Feel free to reach out and let me know which facts you want to see in the next edition.

Please be kind enough to leave a review about this book on Amazon. Your opinion will help me make sure that I hit the mark with you—my reader—and improve, or make changes, where needed.

Afterword

Thank you for reading Better Than Balderdash. If you have enjoyed what you've learned in this book, I hope you'll consider taking a moment to write a review on the retail platform in which you have purchased.

Book reviews are an important part of the process, especially for small publishers. When you write a positive review of a book you've enjoyed, it encourages others to choose to read that book too. It also makes the author feel really good!

QUICK LINKS

Thank you for supporting this small publisher!

Contact the author at support@owenjanssen.com, or visit his website at https://owenjanssen.com/

Amazon Quick Review Links

U.S: https://bit.ly/BTB_US

U.K: https://bit.ly/BTB_UK

Canada: https://bit.ly/BTB_CA

Australia: https://bit.ly/BTB_AU

DON'T FORGET YOUR GIFT!

As a thank you gift to my readers, I have a little surprise I hope you will enjoy...

A FREE Copy of one of our newest and most exciting books! *"WORLD WONDERS: A Captivating Compilation Of Random Trivia, Fascinating Facts, And Curious Tidbits To Catch The Quick-Witted Off Guard"*

YOUR FREE BOOK – Upcoming Code!

"WORLD WONDERS: A Captivating Compilation Of Random Trivia, Fascinating Facts, And Curious Tidbits To Catch The Quick-Witted Off Guard"

WORLD WONDERS

To obtain your **FREE** copy of *WORLD WONDERS*
- Scan The Code Below, Or Simply Head to:

https://bit.ly/WORLDWONDERSFREE

READ OUR NEWEST BOOKS AT NO COST BEFORE THEY HIT THE SHELVES

Are you an avid reader who loves being the first to discover the latest bestsellers? Joining Advanced Reader Copy (ARC) teams gives you the exclusive opportunity to read books before they hit the shelves! Not only do you get to enjoy the excitement of being among the first to read new releases, but you also have the chance to provide valuable feedback to authors and publishers, helping to shape the final version of the book. The best part is, you'll receive each and every single one for *free*. So, if you want to be at the forefront of the literary world and have a say in the next big

thing, sign up to our ARC team today!

UPCOMING ARC

Scan the upcoming code for details. Or, simply head to

https://owenjanssenarc.com/

ABOUT THE AUTHOR

Owen Janssen moved to the United States from Holland, where his father was a professor, when he was two years old. His family loved traveling and he has crisscrossed the whole country (and part of the world) with them.

Owen has a love of random trivia, technology, and educational matters in general. He also has a guilty pleasure of enjoying pop culture and the occasional karaoke night. He and his family still travel during summer vacations; from Disney World to going back to Holland, and he still can't get enough of all the sights he can find.

Contact the author at support@owenjanssen.com, or visit his website at www.owenjanssen.com

OWEN JANSSEN

ALSO BY

More by Owen Janssen

Better Than Balderdash: The Ultimate Collection of Incredible True Stories, Intriguing Trivia, and Absurd Information You Didn't Know You Needed

https://books2read.com/u/3LNVzN

EPIC TRUE TALES AND CRAZY STORIES: A genuinely hilarious book of outrageous events, entertaining world history, and funny true stories for adults! With humorous questions and answers throughout

https://books2read.com/u/3k22WN

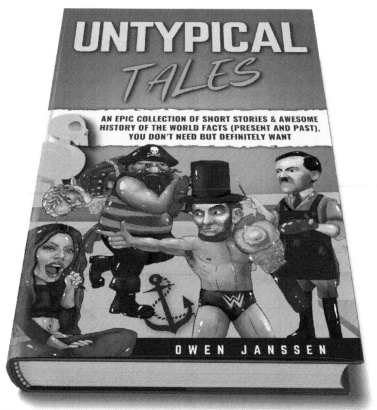

Untypical Tales: An Epic Collection of Short Stories & Awesome History of The World Facts (Present and Past), You Don't Need But Definitely Want

https://books2read.com/u/4NooaY

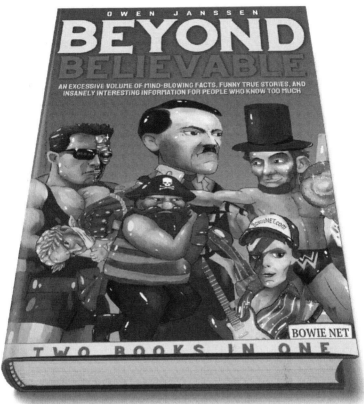

BEYOND BELIEVABLE: An Excessive Volume of Mind-blowing Facts, Funny True Stories, and Insanely Interesting Information for People Who Know Too Much:

TWO BOOKS IN ONE

https://books2read.com/u/bryyWM

THANKS FOR READING!

Manufactured by Amazon.ca
Bolton, ON

34738940R00079